THE FIRST SERGEANT:
... an introduction ...

by Bobby Owens, CSM (RET)
Michael A. Muñoz-Torres, ISG (RET)

The First Sergeant
. . . an introduction . . .

ISBN Number: 1-884308-26-00
Printed in the United States of America.

<u>Books by Bobby Owens</u>

* THE STAR AND THE WREATH

* THE DIAMOND

* THE GRAY AREA

* SQUAD LEADER

* PLATOON SERGEANT

* FIRST SERGEANTS SPOUSE'S NOTES

* THE COMMAND SERGEANT MAJOR

. . . An Introduction . . .

Acknowledgment:

The Almighty God

... and to all who has worn "the diamond."

The
First Sergeant:
... an introduction ...

Table of Contents

Introduction

Commanders are not normally expected to have an expanded knowledge of the diamond wearer's implied duties. Knowing the diamond wearers' responsibilities and requirements will facilitate the commander's ability to command. In time and with experience the commander will realize that many of these tasks are derived from the commander's own specified duties, responsibilities or requirements. The first sergeant allocates time and coordinates learning opportunities with the commander for development purposes. Someday this commander will be a senior leader, who will need to understand the implied task's agenda of an enlisted soldier. New commanders often come to the job thinking that the first sergeant is awaiting their directives before any actions are initiated. The diamond wearer must quickly educate the new commander by explaining the interconnection of their duties, requirements and responsibilities.

Enlightened first sergeants know that the shroud of mystique that embodies the noncommissioned officer corps can never be completely explained to the commissioned officer corps. The diamond wearer must take every opportunity to train, coach, mentor and develop the members of the unit. A great deal of information about the enlisted implied tasks' agenda can be ingested by the commander in bits and pieces from the diamond wearer. The commander must understand above all else how the duties, requirements, and responsibilities of the command team interact in support of each other's role requirements.

... two-way dependency ...

It is the first sergeant's responsibility to ensure the commander understands that by allowing him or her the freedom to execute the implied tasks' agenda does not reduce any of the commander's command authority. Actually, it is enhanced. It must be explained to the commander that it is a two-way dependency when the first sergeant's years of experience are relied upon to maintain the routine of the military routine. Such simple military procedures (chapter action, flagging soldier records, NCOERs, etc.), are often seen as too complicated and difficult. The diamond wearer's ability allows the faster review of NCOERs rather than someone trying to compare NCOER to AR 623-205 while reviewing it. Therefore, the diamond wearer is relied upon by the commander and the units' leadership groups to prevent the routines from becoming complicated.

... understanding the content ...

The first sergeant attuned to the requirements of the unit guides the officers in understanding the contents of the noncommissioned officer's implied agenda. In addition to derive developmental benefits from the interaction between the two corps, it projects the idea that the noncommissioned officer, to a great degree, is in control of individual training tasks and self-development efforts. It is a statement that the required assessment of the soldier's proficiency level has been made and follow-on training is being incorporated into the long range planning. It is also a statement that the quality of collective training will only be realized if the noncommissioned officers are allowed to execute the implied training tasks' portion of their implied tasks' agenda. The contents of the noncommissioned officer's implied tasks' agenda does not embrace any mysticism.

3

The first sergeant possess the skills that underpin attributes that characterize the diamond wearer's ability to facilitate planning the unit's efficiency. What is more important is that it provides purpose and motivates several different levels of soldier's development. Just how does the diamond wearer do this? He or she does this by the conducting of a series of positive activities. These activities seek to engender cooperation, expediency, integrity, consistency, efficiency. They promote other skills needed to enhance the unit's performance. While demonstrating solidarity and professional balance, the diamond wearer creates courses and seminars designed to help officers to understand the contents of the noncommissioned officer's implied agenda.

There is no enlisted leadership position is the Army that is more rewarding and influencing than that of the first sergeant's position. The first sergeant's position interpersonal requirements are so much more extensive than those of other enlisted leadership positions. It is the diamond wearer who transforms the enlisted leadership interpersonal inputs which characterizes the basic leadership process. The wearer establishes the content in which the enlisted leadership groups must operate. Then it is the wearer who attaches meaning to these interpersonal inputs for the officers.

It is the enlightened diamond wearer who exerts that powerful positive influence. He or she provides stability, regulates behaviors to conform, fastens proficiency, challenges everyone to grow and develop (ensures future availability of competent leaders), and selects unit personnel for professional development courses. Anything that tears at the proficiency, morale, operational, the esprit-de-corps, or administrative fabric of the unit are in direct conflict with the diamond wearer. The commander and the wearers are the central figures in the unit. The requirements for competency, the obligation to adhere to standards and the spirit of disciplines to share hardships and successes, and to sustain the conditions for trust are but a few of the items that must be embraced. If these things were understood by the members of the unit, conflict would be minimized. These are the elements or the strands that hold the inner unit together.

The diamond wearer's burden is to do all within the wearer's power to increase the likelihood that the unit's leadership groups will adopt and internalize the values' systems. It reduces the need to punish, control or to demand compliance and highlights the interpersonal methods required to be performed as part of this enlightened leadership position.

The wearer makes common unit experiences as widespread as possible so that all who are exposed to similar challenges (as part of the development structure) benefits from the exposure (lessons learned). Enlightened future enlisted leaders will come forth from units with enlightened diamond wearers.

There is no book that could be written that could enumerate or encompass the diamond wearer's awesome abilities to positively influence all those that come in contract with them. Success hinges a great deal on the commander acknowledging that the diamond wearer is the unit's catalyst. It is the first sergeant who creates a spark when or where there is none, establishing or developing when required, attacking and or praising to accommodate the situation. The diamond wearer's position is a vast collection of books; field manuals, technical manuals, Department of Defense Regulations, Reserve Regulations, Guards Regulations, Army Regulations, other military publication, and civilian publication. They support the diamond wearer's efforts to complete required doing tasks (DTs), direct supervising and supporting

5

tasks (DSSTs) and the follow-on supervising and support tasks (FSSTs).

The diamond wearer over the course of a career commits much of this information to memory. However, the wearer maintains a library to assist in the performance of the mentoring requirements. The regulation mandates copies of AR 623-205 be made available to the noncommissioned officers.

-The Diamond Theme -

"The diamond wearer's competency skills
must be developed and practiced long before the wearer
assumes this position of great responsibility."

CHAPTER ONE

SELECTION

Selection:

The civilian job's market requires a brief and concise account of one's life experiences, education, talents, etc. in the form of a resume. The interview process requires that specific qualities be assessed and evaluated. Jobs are obtained in part based upon the applicant's ability to express and explain how the required job attributes not contained on the resume will be accomplished. The abilities to perform and having the required skills are laid out at the time of the interview. The truth is that the civilian job market wants to confirm the actual personal qualities, skills and knowledge that the interviewee has up front.

The military adjusts more in time with the individual's with growth and development of their knowledge and experiences. The perspective candidates who don't possess the required background must demonstrate that their lack of certain skills and knowledge must not be the grounds for denial but for growth. Therefore, the military interviewer must have the right questions to identify the strengths and limitations of the position seeker. The interviewer must make a concrete and honest decision that the lack thereof (qualities) can later be acquired and reviewed.

Certain qualities are required of any position, civilian or military, but few occupations require of the individual to have as much responsibility as the military does of the first sergeant's position. The first sergeant's position is the axis around which the psychological, physical, the soldier's organizational life, family inclusions, and activities of the unit evolves and are limited. The leader interviewing a candidate must take note of certain qualities that are absolutely necessary to perform the duties and responsibilities of the first sergeant. Those sought-after qualities that may be lacking require that the leader conducting the interview take action. The interviewer must assume the responsibility and ensure that the first sergeant's development program includes methods to overcome the shortcomings identified during the interview.

... creating a development program ...

Identified shortcomings so identified during the interview process provide the command sergeants major the necessary and critical insight to personally tailor the first sergeant's development program that meets all the position's requirements. The lack of a specific desired quality is not the sole justification for rejecting an otherwise most qualified soldier. The interview involves an assessment process by which personal qualities are examined. The one goal of the interview should be to seek out those lacking qualities of all the interviewed candidates. The senior leadership must then take an active role and responsibility in bringing the selected individual up to the desired standard. The senior leader conducting the interview must have and know the necessary skills, knowledge, and attitude that require senior level intervention.

... unit profiles ...

The first sergeant's modus operandi upon entry into a new unit is based on the higher command's pronouncement of the units' profiles. These include the units psychological, discipline, morale, proficiency, esprit-de-corps, ethical, leadership, fellowship, and ethnic profiles. In addition the first sergeant must examine his or her own personal standards based on the intuitive feel for what qualities are present and must be nurtured. As the new first sergeant prepares to assume the duty position, the first sergeants' entry requires immediacy with assessment and action especially if the predecessor had problems putting a leadership agenda together. The larger and more complex the unit, the less time the new first sergeant has to assess and act. The status of the units' profiles drive the contents of the new diamond wearer's leadership agenda.

Therefore, there is no study up period for the first sergeant. The first sergeant must be ready to swing into action, identifying the crystal balls (the ones that can not be dropped) and the rubber balls (occasionally one can fall). The first sergeant understands that the unit's unseen psychological stability requires his or her immediate attention. The first few days of what happens or fails to happen are more critical to the wearer than to the unit. The diamond wearer in the process of assessing the unit must realize that he or she is also being assessed by the unit. The traits of leadership are on display emanating from the diamond wearer's tact, judgment, decisiveness, enthusiasm, etc. The subordinate enlisted population are developing their own mental image of how the first sergeant exercises these characteristics and traits.

... unit's internal systems ...

The unit's internal systems that identify and enhance its profiles must be assessed and the quality certified by the diamond wearer. Those systems that are within standards and in tolerance according to their design need only to be monitored. The systems that require repair should be fixed and brought back to standards. External expertise is requested by the diamond wearer for those systems that require it. The wearer knows that being too proud to request assistance is foolhardy. The wearer also redirects focus and attention from his or her position to the unit's internal systems. The wearer must never allow the unit to be subordinated to any leadership position. The outstanding qualities of the unit are the jewels in the command team's crown.

... effectiveness indicators ...

The diamond wearer equally focuses on both the objective and subjective combat effectiveness indicators to obtain as much knowledge about these two factors. This information provides the base from which the unit's guidance devices (instructions, directives, policies, classes, training planning, etc.) will emerge. The objective combat effectiveness indicators supports the subjective combat effectiveness indicators with having the authorized personnel and equipment to accomplish the mission. The wearer knows that insight is gained by keeping abreast of these two significant factors. This insight will be processed until the wearer departs the unit. The wearer must know the critical personnel and equipment requirements before change can be effected. Changes to the unit's profiles are driven by the diamond wearers understanding of these two factors.

... as the wheel turns ...

The diamond wearer soon concludes that the first few weeks of the assignment are the most taxing. This is because of the intensive process of assessing, identifying, revamping, and monitoring all the internal operations of the unit. In addition, the diamond wearer also directs his or her attention to those systems outside the unit (the external world). All of these actions are ongoing. Family problems continue to pour in. Letters of indebtedness fill the in-box. Unit detail requirements must be planned. UCMJ actions must be completed. NCOERs are near to being late and must be completed. The list seems unending at times. Quality management and leadership are not easy, and were never meant to be. Once the wearer has a good understanding of the unit's equipment and personnel status, he or she is then better prepared. They are then able to understand and relate the

11

morale, esprit-de-corps, the discipline, and the proficiency to determine the unit's profiles. The sound knowledge of the unit's internal operational status will lend itself to facilitating the commander's ability.

... hard but not insensitive ...

The first sergeant has to be as hard as the diamond he or she wears while understanding and appreciating the beauty that draws many to want to wear the diamond. The hardness in support of the ideals that make the unit's personnel feel an attachment that always ensures that the unit's missions will be accomplished expeditiously and expediently. It is then safe to say that the first sergeant generates a kind of spirit. This spirit or attitude causes those in his or her charge to also ignite and glow with soldier power as a result of that radiating spirit from the first sergeant's personal stores.

It is the power of this diamond spirit that is able to act and react to the unit as a whole. It responds to the influencing force that affects its members. They are treated as individuals who share births, deaths, marriages, promotions, demotions, relief's, transfers, financial problems, marital problems, and personal betrayals. It also treats them as members of a collective body that have unit field exercises, tragedy involving members of the unit, sudden relief of the commander, unit award, unit inspection failure, etc.

The characteristics of the diamond also lend to further explanation in support of the qualities that must be possessed by the wearer. Its beauty must not harbor pride, prejudices, selfishness, conceit, ideas of personal gain at the expense of others, egotism, etc. The diamond wearer, foremost, takes stock of all leadership qualities that are to embody every leader in the unit including the wearer. The diamond does not exempt the wearer. It demands an additional burden of expanded trust. The wearer who camouflages herself or himself using the spirit of the diamond is among the worst of persons.

It is from the spirit of the diamond that radiates a force. This force inspires, motivates, encourages, enhances, and empowers the members to share commitment, compassion and join the spirit of the diamond in most military endeavors. It is from the diamond weaver's reserves of energy and optimism that those who follow draw strength. It is from the first sergeant's spirit of the diamond that the unit personnel find inspiration. The commander too is allowed from time to time to tap this reserve of energy.

... developmental lesson in motion ...

The first sergeant's charter, as compared to other enlisted leaders, is a vast charter that contains a wide variety of unwritten duties and responsibilities. The top soldier in a unit has normally been in the service long enough to have gained much knowledge and experiences that allows the flexibility in the first sergeant's position. The directed and specified duties must be kept to a minimum. It is from the implied duties' agenda that the developed strengths of the first sergeant are drawn.

The diamond wearer must have had a challenging developmental career up to this point. A career filled with strong mentors. Progression through the ranks that has exposed him or her to human relationship problems, environmental problems, and administrative challenges. A vast exposure to situations and circumstance that require a great deal of training management. If his or her career has been well developed then by the time this soldier

13

reaches this position, the implied tasks come naturally and with the level of confidence required of the position.

The properly functioning first sergeant is a developmental lesson in motion to all the junior enlisted soldiers desiring to attain that position. Accomplishing the mission, whatever that mission may be is all attributed to those stages through which the first sergeant has gone. The development of a first sergeant starts with a civilian transformed in thought from an individualist to one who knows the value of both individualism and collectivism. The civilian transformation to a physically and mentally well trained, well disciplined soldier is the genesis of a well rounded first sergeant.

The progression through the rank from positions of high directed and specified duties to a high implied duty's position requires that the entire education, training, and developmental base be focused. The focal point must be on producing top quality soldiers whose implied task selections are pre-enhanced by the knowledge gained at the junior leadership level. There is one valuable lesson that must be understood by the entire enlisted leadership group. The lesson is that a first sergeant who has undergone these developmental stages and understands all the growing pains is in the best position to influence the development of all subordinate leaders.

The first sergeant is the nucleus around whom the activities of the unit's enlisted corps functions. All and any actions or activities involving an enlisted soldier must involve the first sergeant. The degree of involvement is subject for discussion. That degree is determined to a large extent by the first sergeant's assessment of the subordinate leaders' abilities to accomplish the action(s). Directly or indirectly, the action will incorporate the first sergeant's DSSTs or FSSTs.

14

... relief from time to time ...

The myriad list of activities that a first sergeant must accomplish can be mind-staggering. He or she has to monitor, inspect, mentor, establish, revamp, assess, evaluate, manage, maintain, emphasize, plan, process, arrange, review, and investigate among other things. Despite all this, the realization is that the first sergeant is of human stuff and requires relief from time to time. To casual observers, it may seem that the diamond wearer possesses a super-human ability to withstand high levels of stress, however the first sergeant is not invincible. The experienced diamond wearer knows when to stand back with hands off with the idea of determining what functions only because of the wearer's presence and involvement. The true quality of the first sergeant lies in his or her ability to be gone and the unit or activity continues its quality operations.

The first sergeant ensures that there are trained follow-on enlisted leaders. These are leaders, who are willing to step forward and demonstrate to some degree their skills and knowledge required to manage and lead the unit. The experienced first sergeant affords these future leaders the opportunity to gain knowledge and experience as often as possible. He or she provides them with first hand experience by use of a "Hands-on" technique. The first sergeant mentors them as they "Do it." This is an integral step in the progression of developing future capable leaders.

...enumeration not required...

The first sergeant's implied duties are not posted by the unit commander's decree. The most qualified soldier who needs the commander to enumerate implied duties should be denied the opportunity to wear the diamond. The symbol has always been entrusted to the best of the noncommissioned officer corps and it is they who composed the listing of implied tasks. Anything and everything that needs to be done at a specific time or place by specific persons for a specific reason is contained on the first sergeant's list of duties. The diamond wearer is psychologically in contact with the entire unit using the stores of collected data about the unit (combat effectiveness indicators). The wearer is a master at making the comparisons of indicators to the unit's status and should always be given the latitude to carry out the task of adjusting.

The first sergeant in essence work for the unit commander, nonetheless, the commander must allow the first sergeant to lead within the spirit of the enlisted corps. The commander who controls the duty activities of the first sergeant stifles the unit's inner spirit and at worst create conflicts with the first sergeant. The first sergeant who finds himself or herself in such situation explains to the unit commander that he or she can not command and be first sergeant. Commanding in itself is full-time. The first sergeant uses all the necessary respect and tact when conveying to the commander who wants to be first sergeant that the unit suffers when the commander and first sergeant can not reach an interpersonal balances.

... the spirit of the diamond ...

The spirit of the diamond is trained to engulf the psychological being of every soldier in the unit. The many years of interpersonal relationships gives the diamond wearer that six sense that enables the wearer to detect soldiers who demonstrate other than their full potential of soldier power. It is the first sergeant who understands best that drains of individual soldier power diminishes the quality of the whole. Drains of soldier power adds up when considered in numbers.

16

A two hundred soldier company with low morale and skills decay pulls energy from those who are maintaining (unaffected by the element(s) causing the low morale). The first sergeant occupies time ensuring that once detected, the causes for the detriment(s) are challenged. The wearer create situations where platoon sergeants and platoon leaders quickly reach their interpersonal balance (another important subjective combat effectiveness indicator) with their peers (not only within the unit but in surrounding units as well).

... cause seeking ...

There are many reasons for the drain on soldier power. It requires the first sergeant to demonstrate tenacity in seeking out those causes. Morale as defined by Webster is (2a: the mental and emotional condition (as of enthusiasm, confidence, or loyalty) of an individual or group with regard to the function or tasks at hand; 3: the level of individual psychological well-being based on such factors as a sense of purpose and confidence in the future). It will not always be as high as the chain of command wants it to be, however, there is a point to which it must not be allowed to fall.

... proficiency ...

Proficiency, another soldier factor by which the state of the unit is measured. It is defined by Webster as the advancement in knowledge or skill. The diamond wearer's role in this process is identified, after the assessment process is completed. As the person in the unit who connects with the external world (the world outside the unit), he or she ensures that[1] the members of unit are afforded the opportunity to advance their knowledge and skills. The wearer ensures

---

[1] Merriam Webster's Collegiate Dictionary, Tenth Edition

that all the unit's organic assets are used to the maximum extent to advance knowledge and skill. The wearer's focus is toward both individual and collective proficiency. Proficiency directly affects the unit's ability to accomplish each assigned mission in the highest possible standards. Skills and knowledge of the individual soldiers come together like all the combined material fused together in the making of a skyscraper. The diamond wearer explains to the leadership groups that morale affects attitude and that attitude affects proficiency. Low morale prevents proficiency from being completely attained and properly demonstrated. In order to properly ascertain proficiency, it has to be assessed as it is demonstrated. Easy tasks completed at minimum standards by soldiers is a sure indication that low morale is affecting proficiency. Highly proficient soldiers with high morale will always perform tasks to the highest standards when allowed to do so.

... discipline ...

The diamond wearer comes armed with the knowledge that soldiers generally want their unit to be the best. Their unity and fellowship is clearly demonstrated through the forces that they are capable of influencing i.e. morale, proficiency, esprit-de-corps, discipline, etc. Discipline like proficiency is also a good indicator of unit morale level. The first sergeant keeps the leadership groups focused on the need for balancing these soldier factors. He or she ensures that the groups recognize and understand the relationship of their causes and effects. Discipline as defined by Webster as control gained by enforcing obedience or order b: orderly or prescribed conduct or pattern of behavior c: self-control. The problems in a unit are generated to some extent by the lack of discipline. This can be and at times may be a direct reflection on the first sergeant. Enforcing obedience and order or lack of can always spill over into the local community where soldiers go to get away from it all and where they live. These attitudes are demonstrated by the control gained and maintained within the unit.

The enlightened first sergeant maintains the balance in the relationship of these four indicators of good leadership (morale, proficiency, esprit-de-corps, discipline). He or she is continuously observant as they are called into play as the unit performs. The first sergeant while focused on these qualities also monitors and adjusts the unit's leadership groups awareness and encourages them to do likewise. It is the diamond wearer who attunes the relationship of the four indicators within the unit and the leadership groups.

... uniqueness ...

It is the first sergeant's concentrated efforts in sharing the commanders vision and communicating the intent that will cause all the unit's leadership groups to embrace it. A clearly defined goal(s) as explained by the first sergeant gives the unit its form and dictates the way they and the unit interacts. The members of the different leadership groups look to the diamond wearer to bridge those gaps between them and the commander. The first sergeant becomes the catalyst that converts unit personnel initiatives and moves the unit toward its mission accomplishments and goals. These are some of the qualities of the diamond wearer's position that gives it uniqueness.

... professional energies ...

Leadership groups focus their professional energies to some degree as directed by the diamond wearer's bearing and competence. These groups make no correlation between the selection from either the primary or secondary zone and the wearing of the diamond. In their minds there are no distinctions or attributes that selection from either zone may possibly result in failure to bring to bear skills, attitudes, and moral strengths to aid and facilitate the commander's ability to command. It is the leadership groups professional energies that are ignited by the diamond wearer's flame. This combustion then translates the individual training program into collective unit missions. The enlightened first sergeant knows that the secret to success is interlocked leadership groups. The first sergeant knows that he or she must serve them through efficient communications, and the willingness to demonstrate his or her subordination to personal needs. It is the combination of action through example by the first sergeant that ultimately the leadership groups do likewise and subordinate their personal needs to the needs of soldiers and mission accomplishment.

CHAPTER TWO

DUTY RELATIONSHIPS

- **Commander**

- **Command Sergeant Major**

- **Platoon Sergeants**

- **The Spirit of the Unit**

The Commander:
... facilitating the commander's ability ...

The first sergeant having progressed up through the enlisted leadership ladder, now assumes a position of great responsibility. The diamond wearer immediately begins to facilitate the abilities of the commander by instituting appropriate conditions that generate understanding of the common intent. Once the conditions are instituted, the diamond wearer reinforces the structure of those conditions by aligning them with a consistent mechanism that ensure that they remain in force and are enforced by the unit's leadership groups. The best terms to apply to this created condition are effective focusing and involvement. Implementation alone is not enough to support or to sustain the standard(s).

The first sergeant having risen through the enlisted ranks brings to the position a special understanding and insights that facilitate the ability of the commander to guide the unit to mission accomplishment. These understandings and insights are all associated with motivating soldiers. The wearer knows that the formulation of this understanding is critical. In order to effectively facilitate, the diamond wearer requires the ability to communicate effectively with the entire unit as well as installing those communications skills to encourage the ability of a unit to communicate with itself.

The enlightened first sergeant readily accepts the challenge to defeat the greatest of the obstacles to the unit cohesiveness. He or she takes the necessary action that promotes the conversion of personal initiatives into organizational agility. This course of action then becomes the catalyst that allows the rapid exploitation of opportunities that move the unit toward mission accomplishment. The diamond wearer has that ever present implied task of focusing the professional energy of the unit's leadership groups while subordinating themselves willingly to the needs of the unit, the soldiers and their family members.

Some of the commander's personal initiatives will be converted into organizational agility with the diamond wearer at the center of the conversion. It is the rare situation in which the majority of the commander's personal initiatives are converted or processed without the wearer's involvement. It is when the diamond wearer is left out that it becomes apparent that a shadow has fallen over the unit level command team's relationship. In having his or her involvement, it then becomes a statement of confidence, of a working relationship, of interpersonal balancing, or in the latter the lack thereof. As a result of this relationship, much of the unit's professional energy (from all sources that could provide such energy) is never really entered into the equation but nevertheless is critical in that it gives the unit its structure.

> There is always the need to guard against confusing personal loyalty with loyalty to higher ideas.

... complexity of the command process ...

The enlightened first sergeant above all else facilitates the commander's ability to face the inherent complexity of the command process. The first sergeant is at the center of the unit's operations providing the enlisted force with what it needs to combat the elements of understood strains that tends to dilute the effect of command. Diluted command effect diminishes command and control of the unit. This diamond wearer helps the commander to set the perimeter and provide the unit's structure. He or she facilitates the command process by being involved in detailed problem solving, synthesis, reception and integration, the selection of unit personnel for professional development courses, and applying the conceptual ability to relate current action to future needs.

The diamond wearer's well developed capabilities provide the commander with the means to stay abreast of the many recurring activities. These are activities that must be checked, accounted for, inspected, counted, surveyed, etc., so that resources will be properly allocated and the unit's needs satisfied. It is the first sergeant who keeps the routine as routine as possible which allows the commander time to command. The wearer tempers actions with a clear understanding of what is important to the commander's vision and what achieves results.

It is the first sergeant whom first confronts those elements that would tear into the morale, operational aspects, esprit-de-corps, proficiency, or administrative fabric of the unit. The first sergeant exploits unit success and is constantly engaged in efforts to promote understanding and insight among the unit's leadership groups. The first sergeant continuously monitors the conditions and atmosphere that cultivates continued success to ensure the critical balance is maintained throughout the unit.

... commander and first sergeant internetted task ...

The first sergeant's application of implied tasks in support of the commander's specified and directed tasks lead to what must be termed as internetted tasks. One can say that all of the diamond wearer's internetted tasks are implied tasks but not all the implied tasks are necessarily internetted. Internetted tasks like the internetted chain provides the additional required strength to support the unified effort (of the command team, the command team and the unit, and the unit).

The performance level of the unit significantly decreases when there is a change of one, or the other of these company-level command team members. Strands of the intenetted chain that are removed subtracts from the chain's internetted purpose and quality.

The diamond wearer's knowledge and skills personified adds those strands to this internetted chain allowing the commander to expand the scope from one group to another. It is the diamond wearer who creates consistent mechanisms to ensure that the unit continuously operates in a manner that supports unified effort. The diamond wearer is the commander's partner in insulating the unit from unwarranted external and unnecessary internal structural, training or operational changes.

The commander's activities or behaviors performed to stimulate, acquire, direct, integrate, access, monitor, and allocate resources, to ensure efficient use of the soldiers and equipment is purposeful, thoughtful and always rational. The first sergeant assists the commander through his continuous support and timely sound advice given based on the diamond wearer's experience base (skills, knowledge, expertise). Continuing attention to mental and physical conditioning that stimulates performance oriented training is at the top of these two company level leaders tasks lists.

Because of the human system the diamond wearer represents, the wearer is the spirit of that human system who makes the difference for that system.

The first sergeant more than anybody else in the unit keeps the commander on the straight road that leads to achieving command effectiveness. The wearer does not allow personal ego (that will disrupt, create levels of stress) rather than organizational and mission needs to drive the commander's actions.

It is the diamond wearer who is most concerned with engendering habits that facilitate success (individual, junior leader, personal). The wearer's finger on the pulse of the command is the key to accomplishing this task.

The diamond wearer is the one enlisted soldier of this company-level command team, who can level charges of inconsistencies. It is through the first sergeant's continuous monitoring of the unit that examples can be explained involving out of synch synchroneity, any decrease in achieving moral ascendancy, or failure to discharge ethical responsibilities. Examples of inconsistencies, stubbornness, or any other personal trait that would be viewed in the negative (preventing the converting of personal initiative into organizational agility) are safely and candidly discussed without the rise of friction within the unit's members. The diamond wearer's knowledge of the "subjective combat effectiveness indicators" of the unit helps the commander to prevent these negatives from eating away of the morale or the esprit-de-corps.

... command team interaction ...

Commanders, who allow their first sergeants to execute the implied duties, requirements and responsibilities without inhibition, help the diamond wearer to facilitate the commander's abilities to command the unit. It is the commander who must clarify to all the members of the unit that the first sergeant occupies a position of control, importance and authority. The commander should spend a minimal amount of time defining the first sergeant's role. Role clarification is a requirement for the first sergeant.

The diamond wearer needs the commander as the force of authority to accomplish all that must be accomplished in the allotted time by the personnel and equipment provided. The diamond wearer needs the commander to support the wearer's implied tasks agenda to the maximum extent, and only inserting directives where and when required. The diamond wearer also needs the commander to understand that the first sergeant's implied tasks agenda contains some important tasks just as the commander's specifies tasks agenda does. The diamond wearer's agenda must be respected and coordinated. A commander who constantly cancels out the diamond wearers agenda sends the thought messages that the first sergeant's agenda carries no importance. It is understood that every leader in the chain of command has their agenda canceled from time to time. It is only when it becomes a habit by the commander that the practice then becomes counter productive to teamwork and cohesiveness.

The duties of the commander and the first sergeant are intertwined. The creation of the first sergeant's position was not the result of a cataclysmic explosion or a convergence of the top minds of that or this day. This position evolved as a result of the unit commanders needing someone to assist them. Someone to facilitate their abilities to accomplish assigned missions and help to train and to care for soldiers. The Army grew larger and with it the task of controlling and the responsibility of maintaining personnel and equipment status's, all of which embraced the first sergeant's position. The first sergeant implieds (not all), created from the commanders specified, implied and directed responsibilities, depend to a large part on the unit's assigned or directed mission.

> "Drop decision-making back into the subordinate leader's lap (whenever possible). Do not allow subordinate leaders to 'delegate upwards'."

Commander in executing their specified and directed duties, a requirement that still exist to this day, selected the most educated soldier who could read and write for the job.

	Specified	Directed	Implied
Commander	Provide information to the soldier who medical authority determines to be pregnant on her options, entitlements, and responsibilities. (AR 635-200)	# Leader in the chain of command directs that the commander will provide training time for pregnancy prevention by the health nurse or other medical personnel.	# Counsel soldiers long before their pregnancies on the hardships associated with providing principal care or support. # Maintain records of counselings.

Specified Duties:

- Certain military publications state that the commander and only the commander can perform the duty, in those cases, the commander should be the only person to complete the action.

- In those cases where the commander can complete the action, the first sergeant must assist by ensuring that those elements required to complete the action are known (in support of completing the action). The first sergeant's implieds are often sub-tasks of the commander's duties (specified, directed, implied).

- Since the military publication did not specify that the duty would be accomplished by the first sergeant, the first sergeant (because of the support role to the commander) will take an active part in ensuring that the commander's specified duty is accomplished. Support tasks then become the first sergeant's implied duties. The transformation of a commander's specified duty into a first sergeant's implied duty provides the commander the opportunity to command, while the first sergeant monitors and orchestrates the day to day activities of the unit (facilitating the commander's ability).

Commander's Specified Duty	First Sergeant's Implied Duty
* Commander will separate a soldier for misconduct when it is clear that any additional rehabilitation effort is unlikely to succeed (also known as "Chapter 14 Discharges").	* The first sergeant ensures that the unit's noncommissioned officers are correctly advised on the procedures and standards to properly record information on the soldier who exhibits a pattern of minor disciplinary infractions, have committed a serious offense, are convicted by civil authorities, have deserted, or are absent without leave (AWOL). Proper counseling of such a soldier ensure due judicial process. * Instructs noncommissioned officer on methods to rehabilitate soldiers.

Commander's Specified Duty	First Sergeant's Implied Duty
* Commander will separate a soldier for unsatisfactory performance when it is his judgment that the soldier will not become a satisfactory soldier.	* The first sergeant ensures that in addition to the commander's counseling the soldier also receives adequate noncommissioned officer's counseling.
	* Attempts to rehabilitate IAW AR 600-200 is done through the noncommissioned officers for the most part. Records of attempts to rehabilitate are used to support decision to separate the soldier(s).

Examples of Duty Relationship

Note: The undertaking of indepth study of the first sergeant's position early-on by a prospective holder allows for a better understanding of the transformation of commander's specified duties into the first sergeant's implied duties. One commander specified duty task could possibly generate many implied first sergeant duties for that one specified action.

The first sergeant's position at the top of the enlisted leadership ladder, is a low specified, low directed, but high implied duty position. The chart with the "Specified," "Directed," and "Implied Duties" show their correct proportion. To clarify this concept, one must understand the squad leader's position and duties in contrast to those of the first

31

sergeant's position, the bottom of the leadership leaders, are a high directed, low implied duty position.

	Specified	Directed	Implied Duties
Doing Task (those tasks performed only by the diamond wearer	Those duties stated in a military publication that specify that the duty will be accomplished by a certain leadership position, section leader, etc	Duties not specified in any publication but directed to be accomplished by someone in authority to direct.	Duties not specified in any military publication and not directed by someone in authority to deirect. These are more of assume (unwritten) category. They are supported by the leaders' experience and knowledge of what has to be done in order to accomplish the assigned mission
	Specified by: - AR TM - FM, DOD Reg - Soldiers Training - Publications	Directed by: - Commanding Officer - Bn Commander - CSM	Implied: Known from - Experience and knowledge base - Obtained from other senior leaders
	Five Percent	Ten Percent	Eighty Five Percent

... transition to the diamond wearer's position ...

The soldier who has lived the sheltered life has been denied the benefits derived from strong mentors and the experience with demands for responsibility and its associated growing pains of selected junior enlisted leadership positions. The soldier that has been protected from the social-military related conflicts that are associated with the exposure to human relationship problems is then lost due to the lack of critical solution solving skills. In addition the soldier having been protected from the conflict agreement and conflict management development is unprepared when confronted with these problems. To add to his or her turmoil having been protected from administrative and training management challenges, the soldier is totally unprepared and is quickly frustrated. The soldier will then experience a much more difficult transition to the diamond wearer's position moreso than one who has endured and professionally matured through the growing pains of leadership.

The intricacies of a duty (or task) helps to implant on the soldier's mind details that will never allow a departure from the ability to perform that duty (or task) to the prescribed standard(s).

The intricacies and the knowledge of the intricacies hone the skills that set apart the American noncommissioned officer corps and gives it uniqueness.

The Command Sergeant Major:

... growing with the spirit of the diamond ...

The wearer must be the very first to acknowledge the fact that no soldier is assigned to a position knowing everything that there is to know about the position. The wisest diamond wearers seek out the best enlisted leadership sources of wisdom, knowledge, and experience. The command sergeant major is ready and willing to share enlisted leadership lessons learned with the diamond wearer.

"The diamond has a spirit that possess the wearer thereof"

It is through the exchange of enlisted leadership lessons learned with the command sergeant major that information is generated and nurtures the growth of the spirit of the diamond.

The enlightened first sergeant recognizes the requirements to keep the commander (the diamond wearer's boss) informed of the command sergeant major's specified, directed, and implied duties and responsibilities as the relationship between the two enlisted leaders is strengthened. This is especially true in those areas where it may be perceived by the commander that the command sergeant major is overstepping boundaries i.e. in training management, personnel actions, NCODP, NCOES, or other CSM interventions.

The first sergeant's always maintains a professional attitude in the task of being a go-between the commander and command sergeant major's role. The diamond wearer as a professional leader never plays the commander against the sergeant major. The diamond wearer concentrates all efforts on bridging all gaps between the two. The first sergeant draws from the command sergeant major's knowledge and wisdom and explains the command sergeant major's modus operandi to the commander.

The first sergeant supports the command sergeant major in systematically assessing and reassessing the tried and true principles and techniques of applied leadership. He or she provides reference points where none exist, while exerting influence on organizational behavior, and translating the organization's wartime missions into safe peacetime individual and leader training and development programs.

... actions are complementary ...

> The enlightened first sergeant with the command sergeant major as co-defender of the tenets of the profession, safeguarding its traditions and ethical dimension.

These two professionals always temper their actions with the clear understanding of what is important to their commanders' visions and what achieves the greatest operational results. Their actions are complementary and enhance effectiveness as they work through the formal and the informal structure of the command (internal and external to the organization). Their personal judgments and actions define a greater good by virtue of their station or their relationship to the mission and the needs of the organization.

Internalized values and standards exhibited more quickly impel action.

A well orchestrated working relationship between the enlightened first sergeant and the command sergeant major exists as a powerful influence throughout the organization. It enhances effective performance, expedites personnel and training actions. A harmonious relationship affects the levels of motivation and intensifies individual personal efforts. Overall it translates wartime missions into training programs. It further prevents any present conditions that inhibit or restrict total duty performance. It fosters conditions that encourage initiative and discourage any non-professional attitude by the noncommissioned officers. To ensure the future needs of the organization, the command sergeant major and the first sergeant select the right personnel for professional development courses. As promoters of high unit morale, both promptly recognize honest grievances and expeditiously take corrective action while continuing to monitor the indicators of good leadership as well as the overall development of both mental and physical conditionings of the organization.

... internetted tasks ...

The working relationship between these two enlisted professionals is well orchestrated because of the requirement of each to keep the other informed. Meetings, the exchange of notes of importance, the requirements to review certain personnel actions, etc., support an internetted tasks configuration. There are too many tasks to list that could categorize these two enlisted leaders' internetted tasks agenda. These internetted enlisted tasks that can categorize these two enlisted leader's internetted tasks agenda are only occasionally in conflict with each other. The command sergeant major reaffirms that the first sergeants agenda is just as important as other senior leader's agenda.

These two experienced professionals are members of command teams. They represent professionals whose vision they share and whose intent they understand. Both continuously strive to diligently execute all actions necessary to achieve the desired command effectiveness. They use their professional skills and initiative to align their actions with the commanders' visions and intents. Most of all, they bond direction with purpose thereby reinforcing the capability to communicate the commanders' visions and intents. Working in union these two enlisted leaders align and channel the separate wills and energies of the leadership groups. Their collective efforts in unison motivate them into action by providing direction and purpose to unify organizational effort.

... wealth of knowledge ...

The value of the command sergeant major in terms of experience (lessons to be learned) and the words of wisdom to be passed-on to future leaders is the greatest vault of knowledge the diamond wearer will ever open. A wealth of knowledge and insights to focus on as well as an unending sources of tested skills, the professional developing first sergeant focus on the enlightened command sergeant major.

These are only a few of the wealths of knowledge:

- Wealths of training management information as well as the sustaining aspect of training.

- Managing conflict and managing agreement.

- Family information and how to interface with the family groups to achieve the commander's family goals and objectives.

- Social - psychological information concerning isolation and integration.

- Soldier (senior and junior) development information that would take into consideration the learning stratification issue rather than to focus on any one level.

- Information concerning military ceremonies, flags, especially the soldiers' attitude factor phenomenon.

- Information concerning the disruption to normal family functioning.

- Interrelationship of soldier support systems.

> The spirit of the diamond must embrace the spirit of the star and the wreath, the unit, the noncommissioned officers, the community, the spirit of the military complex.

... constant information exchange ...

Despite the first sergeant's full plate of duties, responsibilities, and other requirements, the diamond wearer is in constant exchange with the command sergeant major concerning information on the following:

- Noncommissioned Officer Education System (NCOES)
- Soldier's organizational life (quality and improvements).
- Quality of life (soldier and family), Reception and Integration
- NCOER quality / rejection rate.
- Chapter Actions (quality of packets submitted), NCO's Knowledge.
- Bar-to-reenlistment (lifting of old ones / installing new ones).
- Promotion packets and boards.
- Noncommissioned Officer Development Program (NCODP).
- Family Support Agenda (FSA).
- Family Support Group (FSG)
- Ethnic observances.
- Training management, training brief, training quality, and training failures.
- Battle focus (Development).
- Combat Effectiveness Indicators
    * Objective
    * Subjective
    - Enlisted Personnel Management System (EPMS)

... the Command Sergeant Major's involvement ...

The Command Sergeant Major, who has served his or her years as an enlisted soldier, understands the critical development benefits derived from having strong mentors and having had to perform in junior leadership positions. With this vast wealth of experience, the Command Sergeant Major becomes the source of knowledge for the commander. It is a critical role that the Command Sergeant Major must perform to assist a commander, who does not fully understands the role of the first sergeant or a candidate for a first sergeant's position. His or her familiarity with the duties and implied requirements are the vital link in educating the commander, who does not fully comprehend the implieds associated with the role.

The CSM knows all to well the problems associated with a lack of understanding on how the first sergeant's position is intertwined with the commander position. In addition, the CSM can bridge a possible gap by explaining the "how to" of strengthening the commander and first sergeant connection when there is a communications breakdown. The communications breakdown between the commander and first sergeant will more than likely have as its foundation a duties clarifications problem.

The CSM can isolate the causes of the problem i.e. the failure of the commander to fully inform the first sergeant of the important commander's specified duties (often contained on the commander's support form). Normally, one would think that the first sergeant has no real reason to know what is on the commander's support form. However, the question must be asked, how then does the first sergeant support the commander if he or she is unable to transform the commander's specified duties into first sergeant's implied duties.

The Command Sergeant Major, who is given the opportunity created by a communications breakdown, must explain that almost everything the first sergeant does is in support of the commander's role. The diamond wearer's actions promote his or her success as a commander. He or she can then further explain and provide examples as to how many other implied duties must be performed and be completed by the first sergeant to ensure success. A new commander's desire to take full control of the first sergeant's every action and move will create problems. The first sergeant must be capable of detecting both overt and sublime and be able to explain why this desire is a problem. The first sergeant must be allowed to carry out implied duties with the complete understanding that these duties are indirectly or directly in support of the commander's specified and directed duties.

The first sergeant who does not know the methodology for converting the commander's specified duties into first sergeant's implied duties must rely upon the one disinterested honest broker who can provide the knowledge for completing this task. If for one moment you do not think the converting out is a critical task for a new first sergeant, discuss the matter with the CSM. Involving the CSM reinforces the first sergeant's desire and willingness to resolve the conflict.

The accumulated years of skills and knowledge of these two enlisted leaders never allow the command to ignore the objective combat effectiveness indicators in the training management process. The CSM and the first sergeant know that there is a direct connection between quality training and the objective combat effectiveness indicators. Anytime the elements of task(s), condition(s), and standard(s) are applied (they must be continuously assessed), the objective combat effectiveness indicators must also be an element of consideration.

Effective and realistic training at all unit levels begins with the given collective training long range training plan (mission essential training requirements). The CSM and the first sergeant thoroughly analyzed the training plan. They then give consideration to the two combat effectiveness indicators and command emphasizes to further define the training required. Once these two individual training engineers have completed these actions, they are then able to extract from the numerous individual tasks those training tasks that support the collective training tasks. Once the individual and leader training tasks have been determined, it then becomes a matter of prioritizing and programming the event(s). These two individual training strategists extract from their mental files the intracacies of the selected individual tasks. This recall of the intracacies allows them to better perform training management (planning, monitoring, inspecting, interjecting, reviewing, etc.).

The enlightened diamond wearer makes no attempt to become the command sergeant major's back-pocket buddy but rather concentrates on learning from the CSM's knowledge, experience and insights. The first sergeant supports the command sergeant major in systemic assessing and reassessing of the tried and true principles and techniques of applied leadership. Both seek to provide reference points where there are none. They exert influence on organizational behaviors, and translate the organization's wartime mission into safe but realistic peacetime training programs.

Never do stupid things because of regulations or orders from them.

Phantom's Philosophy

The Platoon Sergeants:

... engulf the platoon sergeant's duties ...

One of the first sergeant's implied duties is to mentally ingest the directed, specified and the implied duties of the assigned platoon sergeants. This ingestion process serves as a quick analysis and helps the diamond wearer to tailor his implied duties and responsibilities to better support and aid his platoon sergeants. Only then can the first sergeant completely carry out the doing tasks associated with the first sergeant's position. Establishing the required actions to properly construct direct supervising and supporting tasks (DSSTs) is contingent upon the degree of analysis and understanding of its results.

The first sergeant monitors the platoon sergeant's duty and responsibility performance, only interjecting and interceding when required. By having a total understanding of the required platoon sergeant attributes (skills, knowledge, attitude), the first sergeant can lend support, to initiate development and organize programs of learning, to relief for cause, to replace, to direct, or to counsel.

The first sergeant's follow on supervising and support tasks (FSSTs) require that he or she also do a quick analysis of the directed, specified, and implied duties and responsibilities of every noncommissioned officer in the unit with regards to leadership. Developmental programs and programs of learning (POL) are contingent upon the first sergeant's knowledge and comprehension of the noncommissioned officer's duties and their responsibilities. It is the first sergeant who holds the unit's NCO Corps in check, monitors performance, ensures that performance is in accordance with its design, and applies the necessary courses of correction.

43

... include and involve the platoon sergeant ...

The enlightened first sergeants who have strong skills, knowledge and insights in management and leadership are better prepared when in the performance of his or her direct supervising and supporting tasks (DSSTs) notices problems. If a number of management mistakes and leadership deficiencies are emanating from one platoon, then he or she can clearly focus on providing the required attention and guidance toward that platoon's leadership. If the deficiencies are widespread, the required actions are then broadened to correct the deficiencies throughout the unit. The wearer then concentrates on creating and maintaining a consistent mechanism to realign the four indicators of good leadership (morale, proficiency, esprit-de-corps, discipline). In creating the consistent mechanisms, the first sergeants always include and involve the platoon sergeant.

... understanding the transformation struggle ...

In the back chamber of the diamond wearer's mind, there resides a record of his or her super platoon sergeant days. The critical transformation to first sergeant, require a role transition that is not easy for some. The diamond wearer must mentally reflect on the fact that like other leadership positions, there is a continuous struggle to determine the implied duties, responsibilities, and requirements of the position. Being the platoon sergeant is akin to that of being a leader of a much smaller pack. The pack still looks to the platoon sergeant for their well-being, training, monitoring, and development. He or she is responsible for their reception and integration as new members of the pack. The platoon sergeant is responsible for their development as they interact amongst the other members of their pack. As leader of the pack the platoon sergeant continuously monitors the psychological interaction, the management of conflict and agreement, trauma management and other various activities of his or her pack. Psychologically, the new diamond wearer must multiply his or her duties, requirements and responsibilities as a former platoon sergeant four to five times to equal of what is now required of him or her as the first sergeant.

The most critical and important of those things that the pack looked to the platoon sergeant for was mentorship. Mentorship is the vital role which endows the pack members with the abilities to replace him or her as the platoon sergeant someday. It is the platoon sergeant who is charged and responsible with ensuring that the subordinate leaders are developed to replace him, her or any other platoon sergeant in the continuous cycle of professional development and upward mobility. The first sergeant is therefore a stratification developer. He or she must be able to focus the new platoon sergeant while providing the more seasoned platoon sergeant with knowledge required for their professional development and upward mobility.

The first sergeant, who is now at the top of the cycle of upward mobility, must acknowledge that his or her developer's responsibilities have vastly increased. He or she can no longer be content with just being the leader for one small pack but rather must grasp the reality that the pack is now many. The enlightened first sergeant never assumes that the platoon sergeants know all that they should. The first sergeant is acutely aware having been and experienced the life of a platoon sergeant. The platoon sergeant position entails a mastery of many subject areas.

The proficient platoon sergeant must know about the reception and integration process, and the soldier's organizational life. He or she must know about the hierarchy of training management and individual training. The platoon sergeant must know about the psychological and

45

social related areas concerning counseling, chapter actions, psychological isolation and/or interaction, squad leader's turbulence and family support matters. He or she must know about NCOES and the values and traditions of both the Army and the Corps that are taught there.

The platoon sergeant must know how to make recommendations for awards, and how to write them. In addition he or she must know how to present them once awards are approved and know about other situations requiring special ceremonies. The platoon sergeant must know the regulation on NCOERs, the writing and processing of these important documents. He or she must know and be familiar with the applicaiton of DOD Regulation 5500.7-R, of the Joint Ethics Regulation, and artificial dissemination. The platoon sergeant must know and understand the combat effectiveness indicators. He or she needs to know about the makings and fundamentals of lieutenant 101, and the Phantom's Philosophy and its application to a given situation. He or she must be intimately familiar with the holy tome of sacred turf areas and the taboos associated with disobedience to them. The list of required knowledge and or familiarity with subjects list is unending.

The first sergeant's training program for the platoon sergeants never ignores the learning stratification concept (training subject matter must be relevant and appropriate to the level of the leader being trained). The stratification concept maintains that for any given enlisted military duty, that it has an associated hierarchy of duties, responsibilities and requirements to be performed. In the conduct of professional development training, any duty or requirement when correctly stratified will allow for the proper enumeration of its duties, responsibilities and requirements for all the enlisted leaders who are to be involved in accomplishing that duty.

Most senior noncommissioned officers in the unit do not like to be grouped with the junior noncommissioned officers in their programs of learning (POL). The diamond wearer always considers and applies the stratification concept when developing training. Much of the training material included in the platoon sergeant's development program is only applicable to the platoon sergeant. In applying the stratification concept, the first sergeant can design and conduct training with the intent of developing not only his or her replacement but also for other first sergeants.

> If the competency is not there, the first sergeant takes steps to improve or develop it. If the commitment is lacking, the first sergeant explains to the leader that there are other occupations in this life that the leader might want to consider.

...The Spirit of the Unit...

The spirit of the diamond wearer must be so intertwined with the spirit of the unit that the diamond wearer becomes the barometer that is constantly indicating adjustments in the maintenance of the standards of good unit leadership. The diamond wearer must be so in tuned with the unit that the spirit of the diamond wearer and that of the unit can only be viewed as one by all other elements of the military community.

Therefore, the spirit of the unit must be encased by the indicators of good unit leadership identified by high morale, discipline, esprit-de-corps, and proficiency. The diamond wearer's spirit must be visibly apparent to all within the first vital hours of assignment. He or she must truly embody the characteristics of devotion to duty as a first sergeant who is dedicated to the well being of the unit and its members. That spirit must always be firmly locked in support of the indicators of good leadership thus confirming the diamond wearer's commitment.

The most implied quality of the diamond wearer with which the junior enlisted population is most concerned is the diamond wearer self-confidence which is strongly paralleled by the display of courage. This display is strongly viewed and appreciated by the junior enlisted in terms of the willingness of the diamond wearer to "fall on the sword" fighting those issues that can prove to be detrimental to the welfare of the enlisted population.

... to focus the unit...

The members of the unit look toward the abilities of the diamond wearer to focus issues. The first sergeant must focus and canalize the unit's energies. This is especially critical when the spirit of the unit is not in keeping with the chain of command, with the community, or with itself. The unit that can not perform its assigned mission in accordance with its design or operate within the established guidelines of its chain of command is combat ineffective. A unit that is identified by the community for its destructive qualities and lack of support for a better community is in- of- itself a danger to the community. The unit that is constantly embroiled in internal strife and conflicts regardless of reasons i.e. poor unit level management, unfocused leadership, a stagnated organizational life lacking quality, or micro-managed by higher headquarters, is not in keeping with itself. The list of reasons why a unit is not performing in accordance to its design can be unending. What is critical is not the list of unit flaws but rather that the diamond wearer's commitment to changing the unit's negative image and direction. The first sergeant's actions must prove his or her willingness to jump into the heart of the fire and choke-off its fuel.

Jumping into the heart of the fire to chock off its fuel means that the diamond wearer must first define the cause(s) of the units detriments. He or she must first establish and construct the blueprint to apply the necessary corrections. In cases where he or she requires external resources or aid then he or she must be prepared to present and take that case to that level(s) that has the ability, will, fortitude, or authority to effect unit changes. In accomplishing these actions, in some cases, there will certainly be criticism. There will be individuals who will subject the first sergeant to questions of his or her loyalty and judgment. Some others will attempt to dissuade the wearer's resolve from "falling on the sword" for soldiers' causes claiming that the cost out weighs the problem(s).

... to fall on the sword ...

The first sergeant must have the willingness at all times to "fall on the sword" when required to support the spirit of the unit for the welfare of its members and its mission accomplishment. It is with a storehouse of courage that the diamond wearer must sometimes face greater odds than those normally confronting the unit command level team. Regardless of the odds confronted, the diamond wearer does not evade the issue(s) when the welfare of the unit is at heart of the matter. The command system makes allowance for some defiance and permits a degree of defiance when the diamond wearer is acting in the best interest of the unit or even what the wearer perceives as the best interest of the unit. The diamond wearer senior rater more willingly welcomes that degree of defiance rather than inactivity when the spirit of unit is at stake.

As always with defiance comes some degree of risk and the wearer must surely take risk into consideration. The selection process of a first sergeant must evaluate the judgmental quality of a candidate before making the assignment to this critical position of responsibility. The selection and assignment of the chosen candidate therefore carries an endorsement along with it and a degree of support for possible cases of defiance. This is not to say that the first sergeant will take a position of defiance just for the sake of defiance. Defiance, when necessary, is a blessed tool to be used in the best interest of the unit members.

The first sergeant always performs acts of defiance using tact and those skills for human insight and social interaction that were evaluated before the assignment to the duty position. Acts of defiance are most often associated with the glass balls issues rather than the rubber balls issues. It is for those issues that are critical to the structure of the unit and in some cases to an individual soldier(s) or family member(s), that the diamond wearer must lean forward on the sword in support. The wearer is always selective when determining the issues requiring sword falling. One must keep in mind, that a first sergeant who continually falls on the sword for every glass and rubber ball issue needs to be evaluated for suicidal tendencies. In addition it should be noted that a command where **"sword falling"** is the extablished norm is definitely in need of some radical re-adjustment.

... no tolerance...

Unit soldiers are normally ready and prepared for the first sergeant to perform the direct supervising and supporting tasks

(DSSTs) and the follow-on supervising and support tasks (FSSTs) upon his or her arrival. They have no tolerance for a first sergeant who assumes this critical position unprepared to take the reins and become the vanguard of their welfare. Eventhough the first sergeant may be the most recent arrival, the soldiers expect the diamond wearer to include them in the long-range planning activities and their families in the events of the Family Support Agenda (FSA). The enlightened diamond wearer supports these soldier's expectations.

It is the immediate locking onto and inclusion of the soldier's expectations into the diamond wearer's agenda that greatly enhances his or her future success. Immediacy reduces the establishing of walls that would normally prevent the first sergeant from quickly obtaining the subjective and objective combat effectiveness information as well as the social-psychological state of the unit. Accomplishing this immediate evaluation, the diamond wearer is now mentally aware of all that affects the morale, proficiency, discipline, and esprit-de-corps of the unit. The enlightened diamond wearer never ever attempts to facilitate the commander's ability without having processed the combat effectiveness information. In addition he or she must evaluate, analyze results and understand the social-psychological state of the unit. These are two key elements needed by the diamond wearer to complete or accomplish required follow-on supervising and support tasks (FSSTs) associated with supporting the unit's growth.

... supporting unit growth...

The focused and properly channeled energies of the senior enlisted corps are the forces that nourish the qualities of the soldier power and activate forces that drive units to superior performance. It is the enlightened leadership of the first sergeant who must perform as activator or initiator, tapping at every opportunity to connect the senior's energies with the thrusting minds of the seeking junior soldiers. The diamond wearer shows the strength of inner character in this somewhat of an admission that the diamond wearer does not possess all the knowledge and skills to maintain the unit at the superior performance level. The first sergeant reaches out and selects the subject matter experts regardless of the rank or duty position. The diamond wearer always puts the developmental welfare of the unit above any inhibitions that would prevent the unit from growing in collective skills and knowledge. The unit is never shielded from growth because of anyone's egos. The diamond wearer's senior rater compares the state of unit's growth at the beginning and the end of the rating period. The question is asked, "What are the significant changes in the unit's profiles?." Unit growth can be accounted for when the senior rater compares the indicators of good leadership to the two time periods (the completed period and the rating period before).

... consistent philosophy ...

The diamond wearer's spoken philosophy is compared with the wearer's performance by the soldiers to determine if the actions telegraphed are the wearer's true philosophy. The enlightened first sergeant is aware that his or her actions are constantly under scrutiny. The diamond wearer must then, model his or her ethical behavior so that its precepts are clearly understood by the enlisted population. In addition the first sergeant never allows the leadership groups to ignore the effect of their own behavior.

"Contained within that symbol of leadership worn by the first sergeant is the complete acceptance of the obligation to be the role model."

Enlightened first sergeants are aware that their actions are telegraphed as true philosophies to their most critical observers "the soldiers." They must always be cognizant of sharing soldier hardships, dealing with trauma in the unit, and consistently applying policies. They must be prepared and properly react to those who disagree with the diamond wearer position as well as in regards toward those who take unpopular ethical positions and stand up for the unit in the face of uneven odds.

The diamond wearer who has always embraced and modeled his or her ethical behavior has no problems discharging their responsibilities associated with being a role model. The first sergeant's greatest of tasks lie in the follow-on supervising and support tasks (FSSTs). To phrase it succinctly, "the unwavering enforcement of ethical behavior standards at all levels never allowing anything less, involves constant vigilance."

... the diamond wearer and
the Noncommissioned Officers Corps ...

The diamond wearer must control his or her noncommissioned officers. A first sergeant, who does not maintain control over the unit's Noncommissioned Officers Corps runs the risk in terms of guiding, developing, or mentoring them. The lack of control establishes a false image of what the actual required standards of conduct are in their minds. This set of established false standards them becomes the standards that they too will use when they occupy the diamond wearer's position. Sub-standards mentoring breeds substandard mentoring which in turn diminishes the high ideals, and traditions of the Noncommissioned Officer Corps.

53

The weakness exhibited by a diamond wearer diminishes the strengths of the corps in a unit where the corps qualities and attributes are strong. The diamond wearer highlights negative attributes of the unit's Noncommissioned Officer Corps if the spirit of the diamond is flawed. The weak diamond wearer will more than likely be inclined to support substandard proficiency and performance rather than seize the opportunity for further development of the corps. This established lack of focus and guidance by the diamond wearer then tends to spread through the corps in the form of apathy. The danger then becomes the fact that a substandard is set as either acceptable or desirable. This tolerance for substandard action is more dangerous to the corps because it then becomes locked in (mentally programmed) as the norm. The diamond wearer who accepts failure without some form of follow-on lessons learned highlighting the difference between the required standard versus the performed substandard is proclaiming that failure is acceptable and preferred not only to the corps but to the unit.

The unit / activity that is characterized by the personification of its failure has at its core a nonfunctional Noncommissioned Officer Corps with a weak diamond wearer at the heart and in the lead of the nonfunctional Noncommissioned Officer Corps. the rating of what success is by observers is subject to various forms of opinions. However, what is not in question is the fact that the first sergeant generally plays a critical role as the heart and soul of any given unit. Some observers would declare a unit that completes its missions but has a high suicide record as successful. Some others would declare a unit that can never complete a mission but has high loyalty to unit and high esprit-de-corps as successful. It is the diamond wearer's inability to alter and eradicate the internal strife (the noncommissioned officer's dysfunctional conditions) within the unit that allows it to function at a degraded but acceptable level. A weak diamond wearer with a corps that has the internal ability for self-focus, guidance and with sufficient course correcting strength will not only stabilize but it will survive. This type of unit can even flourish but not to its full capable potential versus that if it had a strong first sergeant at its core.

The spirit of the diamond influences the spirit of unit's Noncommissioned Officer Corps in categorical ways. The spirit of the diamond is the spirit of the individual who wears the diamond. This fact must not be overlooked nor taken lightly in the selection process of candidates for the first sergeant. It is a candidate with the zeal and the thirst for excellence not for his own sake but rather as the paramount goal for his or her unit that is the prize and jewel of the command. Therefore, no amount of applied institutional training can transform the nonfunctional situations (poor proficiency and performance) into productive modes. There can not be success where military missions are accomplished without devastating the fiber of the unit, without the experience base of diamond wearer to promote those changes.

If the spirit of the flawed diamond throws the spirit of the unit's noncommissioned officer corps into a state of digression, it will take a miracle to create trust and openness. If on the other hand, the spirit of the diamond locks down the framework needed by establishing habits of operation then changes will occur. The spirit must create, monitor, mentor, review, and provide guidance. It is with this course of action that the spirit of the noncommissioned officer corps will find the fertile soil in which to grow and seed. It is with this activity coupled with the willingness and openness of the diamond wearer's spirit that ensures that the command climate is conducive to growth and development.

... engulfs noncommissioned officers duties ...

The first sergeant's follow-on supervising and support tasks (FSST) also require that the first sergeant mentally ingest the directed, specified, and implied duties and responsibilities of every noncommissioned officer in the unit with regards to leadership. Establishing effective developmental and programs of learning (POL) are contingent upon the first sergeant's skills, knowledge and understanding of the noncommissioned officer's duties and responsibilities.

> "It is the first sergeant who holds the unit's Noncommissioned Officer Corps in check, monitoring performance ensuring that the corps performs in accordance with its design, and applying the necessary courses of correction."

The enlightened diamond wearer strives to ensure that all noncommissioned officers assigned or attached to the unit understands these terms:

- skill proficiency decay
- diversified American culture
- ethnic observance
- spirits of unrest
- force - projection realities
- force protection
- battlefield requirements
- cheerless hospital rooms
- interpersonal balance

- noblest of creatures on the face of the Earth
- feedback mechanisms
- blurring of priorities
- situations deteriorating teamwork
- transition discomforts
- needs analysis
- multi-echelon social engineer
- cross-generational bonds

- The Phantom's Philosophy
- artificial dissemination
- multi-echelon training engineer
- family support agenda
- bi-cultural family programs
- point of the bayonet
- reception and integration
- social-psychological isolation
- "Warrior Spirit"
- standard enforcer

- triggering circumstances
- training strategists
- socialization
- survivability probability factor (SPF)
- silent cries for help
- informal contract
- combat effectiveness indicators
- consistent mechanisms
- standard enforcer

The diamond wearer keeps the unit's noncommissioned officers focused on principles, concepts and doctrine which also include:

- How effectively are the unit's training assets being integrated with doctrine and tactical development, resource allocation, and training execution?

- Developing and practicing training habits that will be used in battle.

- Never under estimate the importance of sustainment training. Keeping the training foundation solid, while adding additional layers of knowledge.

"The first sergeant has developed the art of conceptualizing multi-echelon training events. Now the tasks are to communicate those learnings to all the leadership groups."

... other leadership challenges...

The diamond wearer must always be prepared to meet certain other leadership challenges. This fact is especially true in that there are other responsibilities and requirements that he or she may have to perform. These are not normally part of his or her normal activities agenda. Those tasks normally performed by a first sergeant can be:

• Occupying the command sergeant major's position in the organization. This is in light of the fact that the command sergeant major may be away on a Department of the Army Selection Board, courts martial duty, leave, in transition of assignments, or other reasons requiring his or her absence. The seasoned first sergeant knows that the best solution to this eventuality is to be prepared to undertake the CSM tasks. If required to do so, the diamond wearer must focus a small amount of attention and time on the duties, responsibilities and requirements of the CSM. While in most cases, this responsibility is normally performed by the command's most senior first sergeant, the CSM may designate someone else as the means to provide them leadership training and experience. The diamond wearer most likely to be designated to "sit in" for the CSM must stay attuned to the CSM's activities by receiving frequent briefings. The CSM's doing tasks (those tasks performed only by the CSM) will provide the first sergeant the necessary future insights about this elusive duty position. The reference to elusive must be considered when comparing the number of command sergeants major positions versus the number of first sergeants' positions.

• Supervising and instructing the members of the organization's honor guard in preparation for a memorial service. The diamond wearer must have a complete working knowledge of the conduct of a military funeral service and a memorial service.

- Planning, organizing and supervising the formulation of a formal dinner. Collect and study the numerous bits of information on the subject from the Sergeants Major Academy.

- Supervising the proper order and honors accorded in the display of flags involving different countries and / or states.

- Presenting the command sergeant major's portion of the training brief in accordance with FM 25-101 and local directives. The diamond wearer, due to his or her familiarity, will find it easier to answer questions concerning his or her unit training. However while in the CSM's position the wearer must also be able to answer questions about all the units in the organization and present a training strategy if required or requested.

"The informal contract for the diamond wearer is full of implied direct supervising and supporting tasks and follow-on supervising and support tasks in small print."

... development ...
   (How well are the platoon sergeants
   performing their DSSTs?)

The first sergeant's follow-on supervising and support tasks (FSSTs) are the reasons the diamond wearer must continuously monitor and evaluate the quality of the squad leader's development. This meaning is quite clear, in that the first sergeant is directly responsible for the platoon sergeant's development and indirectly responsible for the squad leader's development. The diamond wearer is the first to ask what the platoon sergeant's development program in its content omits causes for action incorporated by the platoon sergeant to ensure that the platoon's squad leaders are properly trained and developed. For an example, what subject can the platoon sergeant include in the program when it comes to his or her attention that the squad leaders are using immoderate language while addressing their squads.

Squad leaders are first developed to responsibly carry out their duties, responsibilities, and requirements at their level. As part of their training and professional development, they are also developed and mentored to be able to assume the duties, responsibilities and requirements at the next higher level of leadership. Therefore, the platoon sergeants must be developed and mentored to understand their role in the squad leader development. The diamond wearer can be defined as the centerpiece critical to the scheme of unit leader development.

The diamond wearer must explain rationally that the platoon sergeant like all leaders in the enlisted support channel must be developed upward. This upward mobility requires development at their present duty position level, one level above and must foster their ability to reach one level below in the construction of a solid leadership foundation with a far reaching credibility for their subordinates. The diamond wearer can unerringly postulate that if at any level a leader fails to be properly developed, that leader stands a greater chance of falling victim to a "career stopper." The wearer further points out that when a leader's failure to develop in some aspect where his or her development is of paramount importance that it establishes a failure chain. This chain is weakened not only by his or her lack of full development but also that of a junior leader, who will not be developed as a result.

... senior involvement ...

The diamond wearer knows the importance of the leadership development involvement of senior enlisted leaders in junior enlisted leader's development. Their involvement not only gives substances to the development efforts but also allows for the senior to disseminate his or her experiences as related to the specific area of development. Senior enlisted leaders also monitor trends to determine where the greater developmental efforts should be applied. It must be continuously emphasized that the leadership development is a long and drawn-out process. It must continuously account for factors and changing variables that impact on the command's leader development by monitoring and evaluating it throughout its course of growth.

... programs construction ...

The diamond wearer orchestrates the development programs construction for the members of the unit. This includes the program's specific requirements, command directives for development programs, stratification concepts, subject matter expert involvement, and the frequency of a specified subject to be presented. The wearer integrates the development program into the long-range training plans, and takes advantage of the best times and opportunities for presentation of specified subjects.

The first sergeant takes into account the unit's development in envisioning, constructing, and anticipating the unit's future needs to prevent shortfalls that plague the units. The fact that the development programs and training lack objectives in connection with what the unit collectively needs and specific leader level requirements are where the first sergeant focuses most of his or her management skills and attention in training management.

The first sergeant ascribes training management and leadership development into his or her personal agenda. This action is taken to project their criticality and importance while ensuring that all the unit's leadership groups do likewise by ascribing their personal agendas to proclaim ownership of these two entities. Eventhough the first sergeant embraces these stimuli with personal endorsement, the diamond wearer should never openly proclaim that these stimuli have only single ownership. The first sergeant structures the entire unit's leadership operation into a collective ownership foundation. This multiple ownership of these two entities allows for the multiple ownership of failures and successes associated with professional development.

The spirit of the diamond is in a continuous state of flux as it monitors the organizational life and its supportive relationship in regards to the accomplishment of the mission. This continuous monitoring ensures that all is in synch and keeping with the spirit of the chain of command. Once the controlling mechanisms (the state of activities by the noncommissioned officer corps functions) are in place, the diamond wearer stands in the background to monitor, evaluate and reevaluate, revamp, reward, discharge, retain, retrain, re-emphasize.

... informal contract ...

It is the implied duties of the enlisted leadership groups that support the informal contract. This contract requires the application of a managerial and/or leadership trait skills to respond. The first sergeant performs a dual role by first completing the tasks associated with the diamond wearer's position, setting the example through his or her actions and also enforcing compliance of the informal contract by other leaders (junior and senior).

Junior noncommissioned officers newly inducted into the noncommissioned officers corps all too often lack the knowledge or are not consciously aware of the requirements of the informal contract. The first sergeant, knowing and having experienced the growing pain that is attached to adding a strip, establishes developmental programs specifically designed for the new leader. The diamond wearer ensures that the unit's junior leader training strategy incorporates the social aspects of leadership as well as the mission essential tasks. The strategy includes conflict management, reception and integration, family matters, NCOERs, DA Form 2166-7-1, training management, the informal contract, counseling to name a few of the inclusions.

... live up to the corps' creed ...

The diamond wearer is always conscious of not overstepping the leader's tasks boundary (performing tasks that the platoon sergeant should be performing). This ensures that all the leaders understand that development programs strengthened the noncommissioned officers corps. This strength enables the corps to better live up to the corps' creed. Supporting the creed starts with the wearer grasping the concept and the understanding of symbiotic-dependence. This symbiotic relation means that junior leaders depend on senior leaders to first incorporate and then enforce standards of development. There is no requirement for the diamond wearer or any other leader to recite the creed. However, there is a requirement for each leader to dissect the creed, extract its full substance, and forever apply its provisions in performance of his or her duties as a leader. The single-mindeness of the diamond wearer in leader's development is grounded in the application of the provisions of the Noncommissioned Officers Creed.

The training strategy developed for the new inductees into this time honored corps (the noncommissioned officers corps) by the diamond wearer comes mostly out of the mental recall. This mental recall process focus on what needs to be known by these junior leaders. It is again based on the wearer and other senior soldier's knowledge and experience (lessons-learned). This strategy represents the wearer's performance of follow-on supervising and support task and assisting the platoon sergeant in creating a junior leaders development program. This is an effort by the wearer designed for a level (junior leaders) where the wearer exercises indirect involvement in the junior leaders development. The involvement is indirect only because the wearer's direct supervising and supporting tasks requires that the wearer train the platoon sergeant (directly) in the arts of leadership development.

64

Once the platoon sergeants have been trained in the arts of leadership developing and have been assisted by the diamond wearer, the wearer changes gears to the management tasks of monitoring how well the platoon sergeants execute the program. Diamond wearers do not directly train junior leaders (they can, but they also understand better than anyone that it is much better for the corps to train the trainer). The training of all the leaders is the unit by the diamond wearer is his or her responsibility and critical duty. However, it is the enlightened first sergeant that knows when his or her direct involvement is required in the process so as not to deny other leaders learning and experience and value of how to develop leaders. The wearer allocates the majority of the most precious commodity (time) in the performance of the direct supervising and supporting tasks.

CHAPTER THREE

DUTIES

- Training Management
- Reception and Integration
- Family Matters
- Noncommissioned Officer Development Programs
- Conflict Management

Training Management:

Training management is first defined by and for the unit's leadership, the unit's members, and the diamond wearer. The diamond wearer supports the fact that training management is an involvement of the entire unit. Once defined by all, all is then committed to its success. All the leadership groups must postulate the success of training as defined by all as one of their implieds. Training management is doomed to failure if it is singularly embraced by the commander, the training NCO, or the diamond wearer.

Defining of training management by all the unit's leadership groups in a collective setting, revised and revamped by the group as required; this collective defining interjects commitment into each leader's implied tasks involving training management. Collective defining also eliminates unit's internal conflicts i.e., poor coordination and cooperation, willingness to support other elements' missions, sharing of training information (lessons learned), etc. In essence, collective defining sets the stages for effective training meetings and subsequent effective training execution.

... to look at all training events ...

The diamond wearer whose main focus is to facilitate the commander's ability to meld leader and soldier training requirements into collective training events must himself or herself possess the ability to meld the two terms, training and management. The wearer's ability allows for the rise above training details and views the training cycle in its entirety. The first sergeant is able to look at all the training events and contrast their present utility with their long-term importance and to establish their context and relevance before they are ascribed to the unit's training schedule.

The first sergeant plays devil advocate by asking the unasked questions about training events when all the loops are not closed, about required external coordination(s), about the relationship of an individual training event to a collective training event, about requested resources that require long lead times, about training being supported with the needed resources (food and / or rations to a distant site), about plans for alternate types of training in the event the weather or some other constraints prohibit the originally scheduled training, about rigid timetables that will inhibit training and learning, or about the reviewing of pertinent safety considerations.

The diamond wearer collects input provided by the unit's leadership groups on soldier and leader proficiency on essential task for the commander's assessment. The wearer never allows an inexperienced commander to orient his or her modus operandi to only respond to assessment by higher headquarters or to overlook the assessments by the unit's leadership groups. Teaching the commander to orient on the unit's proficiency in a sequence of timely troop-leading steps that allows the unit to execute its mission properly.

The diamond wearer ensures that all of the training related terms are clear to all the leadership groups. Some of these terms are:

- Mission-to-collective task matrix
- Battlefield Operating Systems
- Training Strategy
- training requirement(s)
- precombat checks
- decay rate
- after-action review(s)

- training assessment
- "Warrior spirit"
- pre-execution checks
- multiple unit training assembly
- sustainment training
- multiechelon training
- battle focus

... training knowledge ...

The diamond wearer's training knowledge is supported by a detailed understanding of the tenets of training management. Only by possessing such knowledge and understanding is the diamond wearer able to take the command's assessment and the commander's guidance, then conceptualize and transform it to create multi-echelon training events in quality training execution (creating combat ready forces which are physically and psychologically prepared to fight and win). The knowledge and understanding by the wearer accomplish its designed mission by focusing close attention on when, who, where, how and what the commander wants done. Only by understanding the indirect relationship of the commander's analysis to the unit's training strategy can the diamond wearer communicate the unit strengths and weaknesses as provided by the feedback mechanisms.

Once again, it is the wearer's knowledge and understanding that allow for the creation of the unit's training strategies and are of paramount importance. The production of training plans that realistically reflect personnel, equipment, training limitation and fully exploit capabilities and opportunities can only emerge from the

diamond wearer's knowledge of battle focused training as outlined in
FM 25-101.

The diamond wearer's ability to communicate the training
management knowledge to all the leadership groups is evaluated and
re-evaluated by the diamond wearer and any other training conscious
leaders having an invested interest in the unit's ability to accomplish its
assigned mission.

... training skills ...

The diamond wearer must posses skills (essential leadership
techniques relating to training management) which are particularly
appropriate to training analysis, assessment, planning, execution and
analysis. These essential leadership techniques judiciously applied
should stimulate as well as inspire all leadership groups to embrace the
commander's collective training strategy with all their spirit. The
leadership groups would then be better able to communicate the
connection between training and the "war," thereby demanding the
high priority that individual training deserves.

The diamond wearer must ensure that these things happen with
regard to training management:

* That all of the constructive ideas, thoughts, conceptions,
  etc. be allowed opportunity for transformation into working
  reality.

* That all levels of leadership enforce their commitment to all
  prescribed safety standards and procedures in support of
  force protection.

70

* That they be committed to an analytical structure.

* That they (leadership groups).....
  - converts training feedback into training proficiency.
  - determine the connective quality of objectives.

* Ask the hard training questions that stimulate and generate questions from the subordinate leadership groups.

... training meeting ...

Straying from the training meeting's agenda will indirectly nullify the purpose of the meeting. That is to say that what the diamond wearer and the subordinate leaders should spend the valuable meeting time discussing will take somewhat of a back seat to other less important issues. The rule of thumb should be issues that surface, that might be consider important but not on the training agenda, should be put on hold and acted upon at the appropriate time.

All concern must get into the habit of concentrating on the business of training management to remove those clouds of doubt when the training plan is executed. In the execution phase, all concerned should have a clear mental picture of the who, what, when, why, where and how of the training. Injecting the training meeting with non-training related issues break down the thought process and adds confusion to the training planning.

"Training meeting are not designed to discuss promotion boards, chapter action or counseling. Their designs must steadfastly be training or factors that contributed indirectly or directly thereto."

71

"If the first sergeant's share of the training meeting time is more than twenty-five percent–that's too much. The more subordinate leaders talk, the more the first sergeant will learn about what is and what is not in unit training."

Ensure that all non-functional issues[2] (issues that could contribute to the training break downs and may not seem important at meeting time) are discussed and that follow-up times and systems are instituted at the meeting for functional issues. The key person(s) (points of contact) for each follow-up action should also be named and required to keep the first sergeant informed of progress at the next meeting or before the training is executed.

The diamond wearer makes it quite clear at training meetings that failure is not an option and that meeting requirements that affect the outcome of unit training success will be the priority until completed.

Another supporting point is that all attendees must coordinate in honest (do not make promises in the presents of the first sergeant or commander for show). Also any promises that can not be kept should be indicated early on. The diamond wearer always gets involved in those cases where a leader gives another leader false hopes that equipment can be used by another element. The status of equipment and personnel that is projected into future training is discussed in every training meeting until the training is executed.

The diamond wearer lays the rules and foundation for training meetings that all participants would adhere to. Training meetings with their defined goals and objectives having not less than a ninety five

---

[2] Non-functional issues should be solved and put to bed once and for all, however, they should not be allowed to dominate the training meeting.

percent change of being achieved is a powerful tool in units led by enlightened leaders. The enlightened wearer structures the training meetings as to include the understanding by all that:

- Communications (two way discussions) will be open with the agreement to disagree without fear of retribution.

- No leader attends the training meetings as an observer. Leader's involvement includes active (personal) planning, executing the training (assess the execution) and assessing the quality of the entire cycle[3].

- A combine statement of the training meeting expectations by each leader and collectively as a group (opportunity to teach the intricacies of cohesion).

- Participants temper their actions with a clear understanding of what is important to the commander's vision and what achieves training results.

... logical sequencing ...

Discussed is the logical sequencing (review and refine). The diamond wearer reiterates that each trainer is a training manager whose training knowledge and skills must include the following:

- A training strategy to improve training proficiency on specific weaknesses.

- How to focus on tasks essential to duty position.

---

[3] Diamond Wearers show the cycles and the products of assessing the training cycle thereby creating a better training strategy. That is training.

- Collective and individual tasks (supporting soldier tasks) relationship.

- Frequencies for a given leader or individual task (plan sustainment training on demonstrated strengths).

- Taking training information apart, establishing quality patterns, and constructing the beginnings of a set of priorities for current or future training (long- range, short-range, and near-team planning).

... into effective training programs ...

Training meetings are used to translate the unit's wartime missions into effective training programs that ensures success. The diamond wearer focuses the meeting time on that central objective-the visible, dynamic, functional link between peacetime activities and military mission execution. Training meetings are critical because they provide the diamond wearer and the commander with the soldiers survivability factors.

Training meetings provide framework to review training information; attach importance to it; determine its relevancy to the training assessment, individual and collective training requirements, and ultimately make decisions.

The diamond wearer conducts the training meeting within the stated guidelines. The wearer knows that training meetings are opportunities for junior enlisted leader's personal exposure to the conduct of such meetings. Therefore, the wearer ensures that training meetings are conducted in the highest standards and are never perceived as a waste of time by the attendees.

... collective statement ...

The enlightened diamond wearer never allows a training meeting to conclude without a collective statement from the attendees of the expectations of what the unit must achieve by the end of the training period. This statement is one of accountability and ownership and binds the attendees in awareness that all must succeed. The collective statement is seen when equipment is voluntarily sub-hand receipted from one platoon to another. It is also seen when a platoon sergeant takes on the mission problems of another platoon as if they were merging into one platoon.

... feedback requirement ...

The diamond wearer also support the idea of decentralized execution to allow subordinate leaders the flexibility to focus training on their platoon's strengths and weaknesses but still observe and assess the execution. The wearer stays attuned to the quality of executed training as part of the wearer's feedback requirement. The wearer is obligated to make special efforts to communicate tactfully to the leader(s) executing the training, constructive feedback.

... providing the framework ...

The diamond wearer ensures that the unit's training provide the framework with which leaders and trainers (first line supervisors) can review feedback and training information after execution: attach importance to the adjustments that need to be made, determine its relevancy to the training assessment and operational requirements; and

75

engage in priority settings for future training. Quality training meeting will minimize changes to the training schedules, changes that could impact enormously on the soldier's legal responsibility to attend scheduled training. The meeting demands the locking down of some events, at the same time allowing others to be projected into future meetings but all training related. It is at training meeting where internal elements of the unit commit support to one another (directed or voluntarily).

The first sergeant is the powerful influence in the training meetings who demands that the elements of quality training assessments be transformed into effective near-term planning. This near-term planning results is the unit's primary management tool, better identified as the training schedule. The wearer's influence helps to provide the fertile soil in which the training strategy is grown and continuously refined throughout the planning process. It is the diamond wearer who does not allow sub-standard management activities in terms of poor planning, poor coordination, poor assessment, poor input to the training schedule, or poor cooperation.

Understanding Training Connections:

... establishing as effective training program ...

One of these days, the U.S. Army will develop a common mission training plan that will provide the training manager with a descriptive, mission-oriented training program to train units to perform their critical wartime operations. The common mission training plan would describe the principal missions that a unit would be expected to execute with a high level of proficiency. A common mission training plan would be logical since all soldiers are basically infantry. A common mission training plan would also have to provide a tactical training and evaluation program that would link "how to train" doctrine in the 25-series field manuals with the "how to fight" doctrine in FM 7-7, FM 7-7 J, FM 7-8, and FM 7-70. Until then, let us stay within reality.

The first sergeants in order to be the great training manager, as they are known to be, must totally understand certain training principles and definitions and be able to articulate that understanding to their subordinate leaders. First sergeants, to provide that training foundation from which the unit's training program will be tailored with the intended outcome of producing sections, squads and platoons that can perform and accomplish their wartime missions, the first sergeant must constantly study to fully understand the following principles. The principles are:

- Collective training actually starts at the section, team or squad level. Think about the division's war time mission if directed has as its base many tasks below company level and is supported by those tasks. If diamond wearers understand this principle, the wearers will then understand why mission training plans must be well constructed concentrating on those below company level tasks that support the division's wartime mission.

- The mission training plan provides training managers with a descriptive, mission-oriented battle focus training programs to train the unit / activity to perform its critical war time operations at a high level of proficiency.

- Deployment assignments, temporary duties, family time, leaves and passes, etc. impact on priorities of sustainment. Training manager must include these impacts in training planning.

The first sergeant listens to what all junior leaders say in the training meeting and then compare what is said in the meeting to the follow-on actions of the leaders. Also, importance is given to what is said by each subordinate. The subordinate leader must not be allowed to conclude that the unit's training meeting is the commander's / first sergeant's meeting. The most important reason for listening and incorporating subordinate leader's input is to be able to maintain a true, accurate, and up-to-date status of the unit's operational posture. The diamond wearer could poke his or her head into the sand and believe that he or she has a full understanding of what is going on and the control of all that will happen can be dictated from the orderly room. The first sergeant who believes that statements is echelons below or above reality.

... management tools ...

The leader manager, like the farmer with his tractor and sharpened blades, or the shoemaker with his sharpened needles, must attend training meeting with a sharp and open mind. He needs to be aware of up-to-date equipment and personnel information, a near-term training plan and the long-term training plan, points of interest to all attending the meeting, and views of anticipated problems. Training meetings should be in themselves vehicles for training subordinate leaders on how to train in the present period, while focused on the short-term training and coordinating and planning the long-term training. Planning for the next training event, while not loosing sight of that long range training objective. Effectively being able to use those tools that will keep informed those who should know the direction the train is moving. Training management tools when used properly also prevent training disconnects while stimulating cooperation between those who have broken the training code (concerning the location of the best training areas, best times to obtain scarce resources, points of contact who can help make things happen, etc.) and those who have not broken the training code.

Every subordinate leader is a leader-manager and these training management tools become a requirement of leadership and a mode of operating. Without the abilities (skills, knowledge, attitude) to understand where they are in their training, to get their training to the preferred standards, to relate on essentiality (METL), to totally understand what their training is supposed to do for their soldiers, to review for subordinates the failure and success of past training, or to analyze the causes of accidents and to be able to adjust accordingly, junior leaders will not be able to realize what training management entails.

... training strategy ...

The enlightened diamond wearer explains the mode by which the deficiencies or shortcomings of training are corrected or at least brought into the tolerance window of the training strategy. The training strategy also incorporates and supports sustainment standards. Training strategies like any other worthwhile strategy must be well thought out and must involve all human elements who will take part in the execution thereof. Also like all the other parts of the training management model, the training strategy must be assessed to determine its effectiveness, revised and revamped when necessary. It can not be stressed enough that the training strategy must be the product of the trainers as well as the command teams. It all must be multi-owned.

The wearer points out that a sound training strategy (one with individual and junior leaders as its centerpiece) searches for all the intricacies that are essential to squad and platoon collective tasks that support the unit's METL.

The first sergeant monitors training strategies through execution. The wearer must also support assessment, providing the feedback mechanism from which grows the effort fueled by the training strategy. The training execution always tells the story of the qualities of the training meetings that produced the training strategy.

... the forum ...

The enlightened first sergeant does not wait until the training schedule is finalized before conducting a critical review of the plan. The unit's training meetings are the forums where all the participants are mentally prepared to focus on the unit's training proficiency level. These meetings are the forums where available resources are matched to the training requirements, training events are coordinated, the frequencies for a given task is determined and discussed and most importantly the attendees focus training events on the METL and junior leader development.

... system to assess ...

The first sergeant is the one individual within the unit who analyze the assessment techniques used by the leaders and the trainers to ensure that they generate both useful insights and identify dysfunctional side effects. Even more important, the first sergeant tracks the training events that require follow-on adjustments. The diamond wearer also expose the several techniques of assessment for leadership examination to ensure that the techniques are produced in accordance with their design.

The diamond wearer in designing a system to assess a training event or operational requirement first clearly defines the purpose of the assessment. Purposes vary but mostly fall into one of these categories:

* Comparing the relative efficiency or effectiveness of one platoon to another (counseling and NCOER time-lines rates).

* Evaluating the effectiveness of a system(s) (individual weapons qualifications scores).

* Evaluating the efficiency of a system(s) (late SIDPERS entries).

* Comparing the behavior of the unit's members with prescribed standards (weight control, family support).

* Evaluating the overall progress toward one or more unit goals (high SIDPERS effectiveness rates, high emergency development readiness scores, etc.).

... types of assessment ...

The diamond wearer explains the different types of assessment to the unit's leadership groups and the application thereof as a thoroughly planned and integral part of the training management cycle. The noncommissioned officers must be qualified to provide a valid, credible observations. They must first understand the different types of assessments.

* Objective evaluation by individual (authorized military occupational specialty, using equipment as authorized by Army authorization documents in prescribed quantities). How well does the individual perform his or her job using the assigned equipment?

* Objective evaluation by platoons (the platoon's personnel and equipment equal that authorized by Army authorization documents). How well does the platoon perform its assigned mission?

* Subjective evaluation by individual (proficiency, morale, discipline, esprit-de-corps). What is the individual's state of mind? How does the individual relate his or her role to the unit's mission?

* Subjective evaluation by platoon (proficiency, morale, discipline, esprit-de-corps). What are the levels of the platoon's subjective combat effectiveness indicators?

* Direct observation of process(es) system(s) (watching individual and collective elements perform given tasks).

* Direct observation of outcome (gunnery scores, high SIPPERS effectiveness rates).

... trained to analyze training ...

The first sergeant facilitates the commander's training ability by using that well honed experience base to develop training and to analyzing the training guidance connection (effective methods of analyzing training in preparation and execution). There are questions that trainers should be taught to ask about their training before these questions are asked by the diamond wearer. These are but a few of those training questions:

- What prerequisite training (individual or leader that must be completed in preparation for the main event–a major collective training event)?

- Are the number of tasks scheduled to be trained realistic to be trained to standard?

- Are there any low-density military occupation specialties on which some emphasis must be placed?

- How doctrinal sound is the subject matter content? (Did the trainer collect the instructional material from a field manual, drill book, etc.?)

- Does the trainer know how to ensure that the tasks, condition(s) and standard(s) are consistent throughout the block of training?

Conclusions: Training

The diamond wearer is able to determine the status of the results of training management during its various stages of accomplishment (putting the grandiose training plan in motion and being able to make adjustments). The wearer knows that proper controls permit timely corrective action if the training is not being effectively executed or proves to be defective. Controls founded on comprehensive and accurate information takes the guesswork out of training management and forms the sound basis for decisions and planning.

The diamond wearer issues instructions in sufficient details to assure that the recipients have a clear understanding of what, when, and how the job should be done. On the other hand, except for uniform recurring procedures and methods, which should be reduced to written documents (SOP, LOIs), the instructions should not be in such defined detail that the recipients have nothing left to their judgment. The wearer knows that too much detail can destroy the initiative of the recipient and waste time.

The diamond wearer and the unit's leadership groups embed themselves in the deliberate considerations of training with the view to determining, in advance, the most effective means of accomplishing the desired training results (individual, leader, collective). Their efforts also involve the determination and visualization of what should be done, where, how, why and by whom it should be done, and how long it should take.

NCOER:

The diamond wearer's comprehensive knowledge of the noncommissioned officer evaluation reporting system (purpose, the correct completion of the forms, the explanation of entries, etc.) and the resulting quality is a direct reflection of the diamond wearer's ability. The spirit of the diamond communicate to all concerned that the substandard completion and submission of the NCOER will not be tolerated or accepted.

The diamond wearer is the subject matter expert on the A.R. 623-205 and is the center for understanding evaluation. The noncommissioned officers have their core knowledge for evaluation reporting, the techniques of applied experience. It is the wearer to whom the commander turns when NCOER rejection rates ascend rather than descend. It is the wearer who explains why NCOERs are rejected for minor attention to detail items. It is the diamond wearer who takes responsibility for copies of AR 623-205 not being available for the noncommissioned officers.

The first sergeant's specified duties as outlined by AR 623-205 are but a few as compared to those implied duties not outlined. It is then the requirements of all noncommissioned officers, complying with the informal portion of their contract, to include every possible implied task associated with the noncommissioned officer evaluation reporting system. One of the diamond wearer's implied tasks causes the wearer to interact with the rating official as a supporting element as long as the rating officials perform in accordance with AR 623-205.

... supporter to enforcer...

The diamond wearer modus operandi must switch from that of a supporter to that of an enforcer and when quality diminishes the diamond wearer has the perimeter that will provide enforcement. The first sergeant must never be accursed of interfering with rating officials' objective evaluations. However, both the first sergeant and the rating officials must understand that all technical and administrative aspects of the NCOER must pass the scrutiny of AR 623-205 and the first sergeant. The first sergeant can not prescribe or direct what the rating official include in a bullet comment, however, the first sergeant can reject an NCOER because a bullet comment does not comply with the AR. The first sergeant must never interfere with the rating official's specified task as long as that task does not violate the spirit of AR 623-205.

The first sergeant implied task concerning the quality of the noncommissioned officer evaluation reporting system are carried out with a greater degree of professionalism when all of the rating officials accept and support the gigantic role that the first sergeant must play. Many of the rating official in the noncommissioned officer evaluation reporting system are commissioned officers. This fact can be a potential problem for the diamond wearer when rejecting an inaccurate NCOER. The enlightened first sergeant who has mentally engulfed the contents of AR 623-205 always explain any rejection in detail. The first sergeant is always prepared to present an NCOER class to improve the unit's NCOER knowledge profile.

... direct reflection ...

The complete control over the processing of the noncommissioned officer evaluation reporting system (purpose, correct completion of forms, explanation of entries, etc.) and the resulting quality is a direct reflection of the first sergeant's commitment to the standards. The spirit of the diamond communicates to all concerned that substandard management (completion, security, submission) of the NCOER will not be tolerated or accepted.

... diamond wearer's lock in on quality ...

It is the diamond wearer who ensures that the rating officials know their responsibilities and meet the qualifications as outlined by AR 623-205. The wearer pushes forth questions to the chain of command. These are the diamond wearer's questions:

86

- Are the rating officials, especially the rater, developing a genuine interest in the rated soldier?

- Have the rating officials completed a study of AR 623-205?

- Have rating officials developed a knowledge and understanding of the rated soldier?

- Are the rating officials providing timely counseling?

- How active is the rater in recommending or helping the rated soldier to seek a well rounded military education by supplementing attendance at a service school with independent reading, research, and study?

- Are the rating officials using all reasonable means to become familiar with the rated soldier's performance throughout the rating period?

- To whose attention does the rated soldier bring the fact that the rating official is deficient in carrying out official duties?

- What is the mutual respect and confidence level between the rated soldier and the rating officials?

- Does the rating officials promote the spirit of initiative in the rated soldier?

Ethnic Observances:

Ethnic (a member of a minority group who retains the customs, language, or social views of his group; of or relating to large groups of people classed according to common racial, material, tribal, religious, linguistic, or cultural origin or background) observances, like a quality reception and integration program, fuel the fires of the soldier's internal flames of loyalty and gives yet another reason for the soldier and his or her family to identify with the military community. The diamond wearer supports those observances as strands of which the unit's profiles are constructed. The unit's ethnic profile is internally embraced by the command team when the leadership groups actively support these observances.

The spirit of the diamond requires that all of the unit's leaders have knowledge of the background of each minority group because of the military's diversified American culture. Leaders must recognize contributions these groups have made to the development of America. The diamond wearer is the key person to providing background information concerning the diversified military culture in which the units leaders must accomplish their specified, directed and implied duties, responsibilities, and requirements. The wearer knows that this embracing by the command team is seen by the soldiers as emphasis on their value as members of the unit.

Positive development to ensure equal opportunity.

Phantom's Philosophy

First Sergeant's Implied Duty

- Institute and / or Maintain Ethnic Observances

DTs

DSSTs

FSST

- Coordinate with the commander to institute and / or to maintain ethnic observations.

- Provide the commander with an assessment of the unit's ethnic observance program.

- Ensure that ethnic observances are included on the Family Support Agenda (FSA).

- Present the framework of the ethnic observances to the unit's leadership groups.

- Incorporate the leadership groups to plan a yearly scheme.

- Provide the leadership groups with feedback concerning the unit's ethnic observances.

- Observe the ethnic programs presented and obtain feedback from the soldiers.

- Solicit the input of all the unit members concerning the ethnic programs.

First Sergeant's Implied Duty

- Examine the State of the Unit's Morale

DTs

DSSTs

FSST

- Provide the commander with an assessment of the unit's state of morale[4] .

- Be mindful of the relationship between the unit's state of morale and family support activities.

- Solicit the subordinate leaders input concerning the state of unit morale.

- Require that leadership groups also assess their elements' state of morale.

- Provide the leadership groups with the feedback obtained from the soldier.

- Solicit the soldier input concerning the state of unit morale.

- Observe for the signs of an eroding state of morale.

---

[4] An enlightened diamond wearer can provide such an assessment regardless of time in position. The ever present elements of unit morale never escapes the first sergeant's detecting mode as the daily rounds through the unit are conducted. The diamond wearer is always attuned to the unit's psychological profile.

... military life cycle ...

Reception and integration (RI), organizational life (OL), departure (D) (RI, OL, D) make up the military life cycle and is greatly influenced by all the leadership groups within the organization. It is the spirit of the diamond that gives the life cycle its quality. It is the diamond wearer who enforces their quality application. The influence (negative or positive) by the leadership groups is determined by the diamond wearer's commitment to reception and integration.

The reception and integration quality often times has a significant bearing on the soldier's attitude toward military life. This first stage of the military life cycle provides the soldier with lists of data that will later be processed in making decisions about military life in general. My early years of military life with regard to unit assignment gave one the impression that the prevailing thought was to break the newly assigned soldier. I was thrown into the back of a M37A1 (old 3/4 ton pickup truck) in the dead of Winter (Dec. 1965) and transported to my new unit some twenty or so miles away. Upon arrival, I did not feel good about the next three years to which I had committed my young life. My reception upon arrival was as cold as the ride to the unit.

The reception portion of these stages should be short, there is no valid reason to prolong it. This is not to say that it is less important than the integration. The integration portion is that part of the process that requires a silent acceptance from the newly assigned. It is not known by the other members of the organization what is going through the mind of the newbee (a name applied to newly assigned personnel). There are many aspects of processing that will become recorded on the mind and heart of the soldier. The initial contacts with people will have the greatest affect on what is recorded, followed closely by how organized the organization appears to be, and thirdly–accommodations. The newly assigned should be introduced to as many of the assigned personnel in the first few days as possible. These names and faces in time will become a part of the newbee's recall files and should not be expected to be able to remember everyone. The newbee should also be processed expeditiously, not having to stand around waiting for someone to sign something, a form to be located or a paper to be reproduced.

Integration, unlike reception does not have any defined ending. In order for the integration to begin, the reception must end. It is the quality integration that transforms the words from the newbee's mouths from "this unit to my unit." The diamond wearer's spirit must be at the heart of these processes. The wearer intervention is sometimes required and if the program is well established and supported, then there will be few cases of wearer's intervention.

... the soldier's view ...

Reception and integration lies buried within the confines of the leader's informal contract and will remain tucked away if the first sergeant is unenlightened as to the importance of this vital component of a soldier's organizational life. Soldiers will find their way through the unit's inprocessing and began their duties even if there is not a quality reception and integration. How the soldier views the unit / activity upon assignment or attachment affects the soldier's loyalty, work attitude, opinion of the unit and the leaders. The impression as attained by the soldier (as to what the unit's attitude is as shown by the unit's lack of a quality reception and integration) will be recorded in that soldier's mental file.

The unit's reception and integration program that is void of the spirit of the diamond has a holler core. A core that does not acknowledge the fact that the soldiers attached or assigned are of "human stuff" with emotions, aspirations, and motivations. The first sergeant's implied duty block must incorporate a quality unit reception and integration program. This program is another connector in the diamond wearer's efforts in facilitating the commander's ability because this is first a unit program then a platoon program.

Therefore, the wearer establishes a reception and integration program where the leadership groups embrace the idea that a new family joining their unit belongs to the entire unit and not just to the section or platoon to which the soldier is being assigned. Such an embraced idea then lends itself to the support of a quality Family Support Group (FSG). In other words, the enlightened diamond wearer designs the reception and integration program as a transition mode to the family support thought on the part of the leadership groups. The leadership groups help the diamond wearer to lock-in consistent mechanisms that support quality reception and integration. The wearer's objective in the establishment of this program is to provide an emotional balance for the soldier and family members in the midst of exceptional stress.

The diamond wearer's knowledge of interpersonal balancing drives the wearer to use quality reception and integration as a tool to support the concept of family support. Families who receive quality reception and integration support the concept.

First Sergeant's Implied Duty

Doing Tasks

Direct Supervising and Supporting Tasks

Follow-On Supervising and Support Tasks

DTs

DSSTs

FSST

- Monitor the unit's reception and integration program for quality.

- Establish and review the unit's reception and integration program.

- Enforce the collectively defined standards for reception and integration.

- Be mindful of the relationship of reception and integration to family support.

- Briefs the subordinate leader of the reception and integration program and the standards to be maintained.

- Analyze the depth of the subordinate leaders' knowledge by asking questions concerning the reception and integration program.

- Share acquired feedback from newly assigned soldiers with the subordinate leaders.

- Direct questions to the newly assigned soldier (s) concerning the quality of the unit's reception and integration programs.

- Spot checks the soldiers inprocessing, matching the program's standards with the actual inprocessing.

- Seek input from family members in family support discussions.

Doing tasks are only accomplish by the one for whom they are written. The interaction of these tasks is between the first sergeant and the platoon sergeants (with some exception). These tasks require the first sergeant to interact with soldiers several levels below the platoon sergeants.

... shared tasks ...

Maintaining a quality unit reception and integration program is an implied task that is shared by all the unit's leadership groups. Much like the collective defining of training management, the reception and integration program must be defined by the unit's leadership. The first sergeant must be the catalyst to the reception and integration program's genesis and revision, however, all the leadership groups must incorporate the reception and integration as one of their implied tasks.

Reception and integration extends far beyond the immediate unit area to reach the full extent of a soldier's organizational life. Once the soldier is attached or assigned to the unit, the soldier becomes the unit. Wherever the soldier goes–so goes the unit. Therefore, the soldier integration is unending (because of the coming and going of other soldiers and leaders) in the true sense. Soldiers who were properly integrated into the unit will properly integrate new soldiers.

Supporting Family Support Matters:

The first sergeant (single or married) has an obligation to the soldier's family members to help prepare them to be independent of their spouses in the military in the event of a long-term deployments. Family support programs should be designed to support, not to provide care of family members. Soldiers as well as leaders must understand the concepts of family support. Therefore, the first sergeant in his or her efforts must ensure that matters of family interest are on the unit's agenda (Family Support Agenda).

First sergeants cannot abdicate their responsibilities to family members nor allow subordinate leaders to abdicate their responsibilities by claming that there is too much "Army Stuff" to do or that the senior enlisted spouses will take care of "family stuff." While in most cases there is always a senior enlisted spouse who will step forward to help in family matters, still required is the first sergeant's attention and complete support of the family programs.

It is the first sergeant who ensures that the commander understands that the Family Support Group (FSG) is a commander's program but the family member must be supported to run it. Other family organizations that are not spelled out in a military publications are sanctioned, as long as they operate within the spirit of the chain of command. Family Support Group (FSG) is a regulated organization that the commander must enforce from the military side (cannot force a family member to be part of a family support group). The first sergeant and commander's involvement give the FSG substance and importance. They provide the required support to whomever takes on the leadership role in the FSG i.e., assets required with which to operate.

The diamond wearer's implied task agenda and the unit's Family Support Agenda (FSA) are internetted in many ways as indicated by the interest shown by the enlightened diamond wearer. The real value of family support programs are often realized too late– when the unit is deploying. High on the first sergeant's implied task agenda is the task to promote the family member's personal identification with the military community.

Family Support Training ....

The first sergeant and all the other senior enlisted soldiers never take lightly the family support training for their soldiers' family members. Never allow the abdication from the requirements and responsibilities with the thought that family support training is totally the exclusive responsibility of the commanders or / and the enlightened enlisted spouses. The first sergeant also establishes the policy that requires that all noncommissioned officers read and study the White Paper 1983.

Organizational family support training must have as its strategy a two-sided interlocking and supporting configuration as shown below. The diamond wearer institute consistent mechanisms that ensures that family members are as involved as they need to be.

Organizational Family Support Training

Senior Enlisted Soldier(s)Senior Enlisted Spouse(s)
- Stressing the importance of family support matters to all military leaders.
- Stressing to leaders why and the results of dereliction in counseling their soldiers on family involvement which creates serious problems for the rear detachment.
- Ensure that every leader can clearly define within his or her own mind the following family support associated terms:
  * Family Support Agenda (FSA)
  * Social psychological
    - Involvement
    - Isolation
  * Inappropriate dependency
- Train new Family Support Group (FSG) members and volunteers.
- Stressing the importance of family support matters to senior enlisted spouses.
- Stressing to all spouses the importance of family readiness and family involvement to preclude the void that is created when the requirements of a soldier are evoked (deployments, long separations, etc.)
- Call to the command's attention when it is evident that the command is not psychologically enrolled to family matters.
- Communicate to their senior enlisted spouse when their support is thought to be inadequate.
- Cheerless hospital room (family members) understanding.
- Train new Family Support Group (FSG) members and volunteers.

... family readiness ...

The first sergeant is enlightened in family readiness because of the serious impacts that the lack thereof would have on the unit readiness. Family oriented soldiers look to the command that dispatches them around the world to establish well-defined back up family support systems. The first sergeant with or without spouse incorporates the provisions of DA Pam 608-47 into the daily activities of the unit and the Family Support Agenda (FSA).

The first sergeant ensures that whatever the unit does, family readiness is injected into the discussion. Training meetings, the planning of deployments, etc. must consider family readiness. Military training that is impacted by family readiness is given priority by the first sergeant and is included on the unit's Family Support Agenda (FSA) and the leaders are given an understanding of the intent of the White Paper 1983.

The enlightened first sergeant selects specific aspects of DA Pam 608-47 that will communicate to both soldiers and family members that the unit is psychologically enrolled to helping the family members bridge the periods of separation that are caused by military operations. It is also this enlightened diamond wearer who ensures that the family members fully understand the term "inappropriate dependency" (expecting the military support system to do more for the family than required while the spouse in the military is away).

Note: White Paper 1983: The Army Family

The White Paper described the evolution of the Army Family: its history, present status and future. It was the first time that information about the Army Family had been systematically gathered and consolidated. In that regard, the White Paper was only the first step of the needs assessment. Future months will be devoted to a continuing analysis in needs and the development of solutions. It was to be a time-consuming process; by given the long history of the Army Family and the piecemeal planning to date, the time was well spent. The Army did in fact articulate a well conceived strategic plan for the Army Family.

This plan envisions family members as true partners in an Army which is seen as a way of life not a job. The family responsibility in this partnership is to support soldiers and employees and participate in building wholesome communities. The Army's responsibility is to create an environment where families and family members prosper and realize their potential. Each of us has a part to play in this partnership.

Noncommissioned Officer Development Programs

"Every leadership group within the unit needs a well developed, well constructed, well supported development program that bears their endorsement."

"Noncommissioned Officers do not come in ready developed modes–all knowing. Some things will be known by some, some will know other things, but all will not know all."

"The noncommissioned officer development program is the most important program that the diamond wearer could establish and maintain."

"The intent of the diamond wearer in leader's development is grounded in the application of the provisions of the Noncommissioned Officers Creed."

"The diamond wearer develops the stratification concept to concentrate learning at the desires levels."

Noncommissioned Officer Development Program:

The diamond wearer's specified tasks associated with Noncommissioned Officer Development Programs are very limited. With that as an established fact, an effective NCODP must be high on the first sergeant's implied tasks list. The first sergeants cannot wait until a military publication is published that specifies who will outline the program to ensure increased proficiency in noncommissioned officers' performance. The program must specify what subjects should be included and how the subjects to be included should be determined. The wearer directs his or her well developed professional energy (supported by skills and knowledge) toward a framework (noncommissioned officer corps) supporting the unit's structure (focused on that which enhance the unit profiles i.e. battle focus profile, social profile, etc.).

... as its foundation ....

The diamond wearer ensures that the noncommissioned Officer Development Program like any other well established and constructed program, has as its foundation a quality knowledge and skills assessment on which the goals and objectives of the programs are based. A quality assessment of NCO's strengths and weaknesses should determine the best program of learning for the unit's noncommissioned officers, determine what subjects based on the identified unit weaknesses should be included in the program, determine the identified subjects importance as they relate to the support of the unit's mission, and also determine which subjects would fall into the sustainment category. The quality assessment would also identify the subject matters experts who would be tasked to communicate knowledge and skills to the members of the leadership groups.

The enlightened diamond wearer establishes and constructs the unit's Noncommissioned Officer Development Program with the thought in mind that the program itself is a training strategy to enhance the quality of the unit's noncommissioned officer corps' proficiency and performance. The skills and the knowledge to enhance the quality of the corps is more than likely there within the unit's corps. It then become a challenge to the knowledge and skills of the diamond wearer of how to best extract and disseminate these stored qualities. The quality assessment is conducted to stimulate the program to bridge the skills and knowledge gaps that are always present in a unit. The unenlightened wearer would stick head in the sand, concluding that everybody knows everything about anything.

Armed with a quality knowledge and skills assessment, the diamond wearer presents the stated outline showing the results of the assessment, both knowledge and skill's strengths and weaknesses. The best tool for presentation is in the form of a program of learning (POL) which is a lot less detailed and devoid of flexibility than a program of instruction (POI). The program of learning's design tells the wearer where the unit is in terms of knowledge and skills of particular subjects, proposed methods to enhance proficiency and performance, and methods to indicate progress. The program of learning becomes a reflection of the unit noncommissioned officers corps' abilities to look at itself and create the events to improve proficiency and/or performance.

The resulting strengths and weaknesses are used as the nucleus by the first sergeant to select and construct the program of learning. The first sergeant knows that all the military or civilian related subjects, that could have shown need for consideration from the assessment, cannot be included in the program. This then becomes a subjective selection process, selection of the subjects with the greatest values to the unit's development programs. Selection value based upon the unit's present proficiency and performance if given missions that are within the unit's scope to accomplish. Hence, the noncommissioned officers development program's connection with unit mission accomplishment. Hence, the noncommissioned officers development program's connection with the unit's short and long-term training plans.

Counseling of a troubled soldier:

Any time the commander engages in any kind of a discussion or counseling concerning an adverse personnel action for an enlisted soldier, the first sergeant should be present for the record. The first sergeant should always be there for the MFR (Memorandum for

Record). The notes taken should include, but not be limited to, the following elements:

* Dates and times of the session(s)
* Persons in attendance
* Statements (that may later require recall)
* Follow-up requirements
* The "why" of the session
* Make record of any documents that were required / produced and the disposition of those documents
* Any time- sensitive requirements

Pay particular close attention to:

- Meeting's tempo i.e. hostile, friendly, conciliatory

- Statements above the head of recipient(s)

- Exchange of information

The diamond wearer always pays particular close attention to the tempo of the meeting mainly for recall. It is of the utmost importance that diamond wearer record all aspects of these types of encounters and the general overall atmosphere and feeling during the session.

... Diamond spirit interrelated with the unit's spirit ...

The spirit of the diamond pulls together the very essences of the unit that is not written into any military publication but only in the minds of philosopher and the heart of he or she who wears the diamond. The diamond wearer is much better able to do this than anyone else in the unit. There are more soldiers in the unit aspiring to someday become first sergeants than there are soldiers aspiring to someday become commanders. Therefore, the psychological focuses of the soldiers are more on the diamond wearer.

... reflection ...

The diamond wearer must be forever mindful of the unmindful silent events and reflections forces that are involved in molding the future of the corps. For whatever period of time in which the diamond wearer influences are utmost in task alignment, the wearer must be cause and affect conscious. What of the diamond wearer's reflection will be carried forth that is of substance in terms of ensuring that noncommissioned officers are developed in the traditions? This question coupled with the soldiers' psychological focuses occupies the wearer's constant state of awareness.

The diamond wearer's experience allows for the seeing and/or hearing of the "silent cries for help" just by looking into a soldier's eyes, listening to the tone of voice, watching the step at quick time, etc. "Silent cries for help" echoes back through the years of development because it is engraved into the core of the diamond wearer's very being. The diamond wearer having been around has seen it all before.

... detection quality ...

The diamond wearer's detection ability of the ever present, "silent cries for help" is not the ultimate; for the ability alone is not as important as inoculating all the unit's leadership groups with the qualities which will allow for the development of the ability in others. The case is never how well developed the diamond wearer is, the real case is how well prepared are those who come in contact with the majority of the unit's population in detecting those "silent cries for help."

Using this detection quality is the one factor that demands that the diamond wearer venture out from the security of the orderly room and into the lives and work places of the soldiers. Normally the cliché has been, if you do not have nothing to do, do not do it in the orderly room. The orderly room is the last place where a soldier would want to spend time doing nothing. Therefore, the tendency is to shy away from the eyesight of the orderly room's occupants. The status of the unit in terms of the indicators of good leadership does not pass through the orderly room by way of the soldiers. The detection of their state of mind is best obtained out among them. Unannounced visit or unobserved positioning (not hiding to gather information) renders the information most valuable to the leadership assessing morale, proficiency, esprit-de-corps, and discipline.

> "The same system that knights the diamond wearer has the great responsibility of ensuring that the wearer is prepared to assume this most important position. There is debate as to who should assume the greater portion of the responsibility in preparing the diamond wearer. My point of view is that the wearer must always take the greater role of preparation in other than academic environments. The creation of the spirit is an all encompassing extraction requirement."

... drains on the diamond wearer ...

The spirit of the diamond wearer envelopes all who envelope the unit, embraced by the dictates of the mission. Every self-motivated and self-driven element, that envelopes the unit, lessens the wearer's need to be directly involved in connecting tasks. This frees the wearer to concentrate on other mission essential tasks. This also enables the wearer to direct full attention to that portion that does not envelop the unit and detracts its effectiveness.

If seventy-five percent of the unit is functioning in its mission well, then the wearer has only to improve twenty-five percent and the unit will survive as mission capable. If the leadership groups and seventy-five percent of unit envelopes its mission, less is the drain on the diamond wearers abilities. It is important that a new diamond wearer quickly assesses the quality of the unit's leadership groups and support their continuous moral toughness while directing his or her personal qualities toward aligning the remaining percentage.

The diamond wearer has to be able to engulf all that the unit is required to accomplish, assesses the unit state of proficiency; meld with its disciplined and morale and push forth while steering the unit's esprit-de-corps. The wearer knows more collectively about the unit than anyone, all equipment status, the informal communication networks, the human dimension, and more. Whatever the state of the unit's subjective combat effectiveness indicators are upon the assumption of the position, the diamond wearer's design is to improve them.

If only twenty-five percent of the unit is performing its assigned mission in accordance with its designed, then the wearer need not look at mission because with that percentage of effectiveness the unit is not mission capable because leadership groups are broken. It is the unit that must be enveloped by its members–that element that gives the unit substance. There is that self motivated element (the members) and then there is that element that is only activated by a diamond wearer who is focused on mission accomplishment. The wearer forces the interaction of these elements thereby supporting the military design.

... promotion board ...

First sergeants, as members of promotion boards, understand that they are representing a higher level commander (the promotion authority) and their unit interests are subordinated. Personnel performing as board members must fully understand the intent and the integrity of quality promotion boards. Since the first sergeant will not always be able to attend all the promotion boards (because they are of "human stuff"), the diamond wearer should never send a most qualified senior soldier to represent the unit on the board without having knowledge of what the board's intent is.

"When soldiers go forth from the unit ill prepared to perform a task that equates to their grade level and fails to perform to prescribed standards - part of that failure belongs to the first sergeant."

A few of the points the first sergeant ensures that board members understand to be ready to represent their units and should be aware of are:

* Evaluate soldiers according to their performance.
* Be prepare to perform as a member of the board.
* Have questions prepared that will challenge and indicate the soldiers' knowledge of the subjects.
* Understand that the board members' performance is monitored by the command sergeant major.
* Pay close attention to the CSM's instructions prior to the start of the board.

... religious activities ...

The diamond wearer's position demands that certain enlightening activities on the part of the wearer be seen in the same light as the operational tasks are carried out. Support the military community's desires to interact with the members of the civilian community in certain life experiences. Participation in religious services other than memorial services help to strengthen the moral profile of the unit. The conduct of the diamond wearer's life is constantly under the lens for viewing by the members of the command. Setting the example extends to this personal interaction as well.

... objective effectiveness reasons ...

The enlightened diamond wearer, armed at all times with critical information (objective combat effectiveness), better understands the shortfall of individual or collective mission essential tasks training when the causes are directly related to shortages. Quality training can never be realized when shortages directly impact on meeting the required military standards. The wearer who is always aware of the unit's effectiveness status can present a better justification for receiving personnel and/or equipment for a higher priority. This wearer, by knowing the limitations of the unit in terms of personnel and or equipment, construct a much better training strategy while developing the unit's long and short range training plans. The wearer provides the command sergeant major (for the quarterly or yearly training brief) not with excuses for untrained status but with objective combat effectiveness reasons.

Sacred Turf:

"Sexual harassment classes do not inoculate soldiers
(officers or enlisted) against the evil."

The diamond wearer expends a great deal of quality time
stressing to the unit's noncommissioned officers corps that stepping on
sacred turf nullifies any leadership claims to any degree of integrity.
The idea of using the positive attributes of a fallen one in attempts to
cancel out violations or breaches of integrity is asinine. The wearer
constantly reinterate that the sacred turf issues must be discussed with
the members of the corps to ensure that they have a clear
understanding of the effects that violations have on individuals
(victims, violator, family members, units, good order and discipline).

These sacred turf issues are brought to the forefront in every
leadership group's discussion by the diamond wearer to prevent the
unit's noncommissioned officers' mental files from being purged of the
devastating effects of these acts of inhumanity. It is the enlightened
diamond wearer who monitors for the opportunities when this ugly
monster could raise its head. The wearer then make efforts to
inoculate against possibilities by stressing the impact of nothing less
than accusations. Even minor accusations require that the wearer
devote time to investigating. Therefore, the wearer efforts are toward
providing the leadership groups an understanding that perceptive
situations can be just as disruptive.

The diamond wearer's leadership input to the
Noncommissioned Officer Development Program are a series of
lessons or seminars relating to the sacred turf issues.

110

Information papers with sacred turf issues as their subjects are part of the unit's NCODP reading file. The reading file is just an additional effort by the diamond wearer to keep the sacred turf issues in the forefront of discussions.

The first sergeant's doing tasks (DTs), direct supervising and supporting tasks (DSSTs), and the follow-on supervising and support tasks (FSSTs) are all employed in the bringing to the forefront, the stressing and the monitoring for sacred turf situations.

Example:

Doing Tasks

Direct Supervising and Supporting Task (DSSTs)

Follow-on Supervising and Support Tasks (FSSTs)

- Stressing that nullification of any claims to any degree of integrity is the result of stepping on sacred turf.
- Be the unit's subject matter expert on Standards of Conduct Joint Ethic Reg., D.O.D. Reg. 5500, 7-R.
- Requires that the platoon sergeants conduct seminars on the sacred turf issues.
- Direct that the platoon sergeants maintain copies of all sacred turf information papers.
- Direct that platoon sergeants report all accusations of violations to the first sergeant (especially if the platoon sergeants is the object of the accusation).

- Ensure that the entire unit understands the command team's position.
- Monitor for evidence that what is being taught is actively being applied.

.... doing tasks ...

The diamond wearer's doing tasks (specified, directed, implied) come off the first sergeant's specified, directed, or implied tasks agenda. While a small percentage of these tasks are directed and contained in a military publication, the majority are the tasks that the first sergeant knows that these tasks must be accomplished based on experience and training. The tasks contained on the first sergeant's implied tasks agenda are tasks worked by the first sergeant and only the first sergeant. The training of platoon sergeants is primarily a first sergeant's doing task. Yes, others should make contributions to the platoon sergeants training (especially other platoon sergeants) but the primary trainer is the first sergeant.

... direct supervising and supporting tasks ...

The first sergeant's doing tasks (specified, directed, or implied) become direct supervising and supporting tasks when the first sergeant's doing tasks requires some degree of interaction with the next leaderships level down. These tasks support the structure of the chain of command. Direct supervising and supporting tasks require that the first sergeant facilitate the abilities of the commander, directing activities though the platoon sergeants, not the squad leaders. The first sergeant who bypasses the platoon sergeants (for whatever reason) in the conducting of the unit's business has a serious problems. If the leaders below the platoon sergeants are being held accountable for mission completion, that act is not in keeping with the spirit of the chain of command.

The supporting aspects of these tasks are just as important as the supervising portion to those with whom the diamond wearer must interact. Supporting aspects come in a wide variety of support forms, depending on the mission to be accomplished. In the case of training, the first sergeant conducts an all out effort to shield the unit's training from distracters. The follow-on efforts by the first sergeant are to lesson the impact when a platoon's training cannot be shielded. Allowing for some last minute informal training schedule changes to accommodate last minute distractions helps to recover lost training time. Psychological support is also in order. From time to time the platoon sergeant needs that also-important pat on the back.

... follow-on supervising and support tasks ...

The first sergeant's follow-on supervising and support tasks (specified, directed, implied) results when a task(s) require that the first sergeant interact several levels below the platoon sergeant level or to perform one of the leadership or management functions (inspect a squad, counsel, monitor, obtain data, inquire, advise a private soldier's family member, survey attitudes, detecting silent cries, etc). The performance of these tasks provide the first sergeant with knowledge of the results that the other leaders should be obtaining from their efforts. These tasks help to answer the question, is the unit's leadership performing in accordance with its design?

The first sergeant's follow-on supervising and support tasks are the tasks that require that the first sergeant supervising and support tasks reach far deeper into the very core of the unit than in the normal mode. The first sergeant exercising these tasks gathers the contents:

the knowledge of the units subjective combat effectiveness indicators. These tasks allow the diamond wearer intrusion into the depths of the unit to determine the "real deal" of organizational life.

The inspection of a squad's equipment and personnel by the diamond wearer (follow-on supervising and support tasks) is far more than an inspection. The inspection is the diamond wearer's opportunity to determine the squad leader's ability to lead the squad (the condition of the equipment and skills and knowledge of each squad member). The inspection also allows the diamond wearer to determine the platoon sergeant's ability to train the trainer. The quality of the performance by the squad leader is a direct reflection on the platoon sergeant's ability to carry out the platoon sergeant's direct supervising and supporting tasks (those tasks that require that the platoon sergeant interact directly with the squad leaders). The inspection is one of the tools that the diamond wearer use to provide knowledge as to how well melded the unit is (cohesion). Soldiers and the condition of equipment and uniforms provide the raw data for the diamond wearer to add to the subjective combat effectiveness indicator file. The diamond wearer visits to the unit well after normal duty hours is the exercise of these tasks.

The exercise of the follow-on supervising and support tasks also allows the diamond wearer the opportunity to learn of any junior leader's negative acts going unchecked, of those indicator of good leadership that are in a downward spiral, whether or not the platoon level leaders are listening to the legitimate complaints, the blurring of personal priorities, and other situations deteriorating teamwork.

> "How does the enlightened diamond wearer ensure that junior leaders receive the full value of all that the senior leadership has to offer?"

Conflict Management:

Managing conflicts within the unit is yet another way in which the diamond wearer facilitates the commanders ability to command. Many potential conflicts are put to bed by the wearer and are never relayed to the commander to prevent the blurring of the commander's command priorities. The wearer works at not multiplying entities beyond necessity. The wearer knows that dealing with these potential conflicts sometimes involve tough choices rather than mechanical application of academic principles learned from the First Sergeant's Course.

... destroy the strands ...

It is through the diamond wearers steadfast efforts to allow nothing to destroy the strands of which the unit's profiles are constructed. Conflict situations that would deteriorate teamwork or deminish the importance of the subjective combat effectiveness indicators must be monitored by the wearer. As long as the parties in conflict maintain the learning values of conflict, the diamond wearer has no need to intervene.

... incompatible or opposing needs ...

Conflict (competitive or opposing action of incompatible: antagonistic state or action: mental struggles resulting from incompatible or opposing needs, drives, wishes, or external or internal demands) management involves the diamond wearer's actions to prevent the eating away of the unit's ability to rebound to its desire state of operation and cohesiveness. The wearer does not work to prevent these mental struggles resulting from external or internal demands (that would be a full time non-productive task; one in which the wearer should never engage). It is the managing of all and any conflict confronting the stability of the unit that reflects the wearer's ability. It is the techniques of managing that the wearer is most proficient. The wearer also knows that conflict if allowed to exist in a state of progressive deterioration between internal or external elements of the unit will take a toll on that which the diamond wearer is mandated to build.

Conflict management is incorporated into the diamond wearer's direct supervising and supporting tasks and follow-on supervising and support tasks because of the requirements to train all of the unit's leadership groups of conflict's destructiveness and value. Conflict of itself is not bad. It is only when it becomes the fertile soil out of which emerge substances that are detrimental to the welfare of the unit. The diamond wearer's proper managing of conflict creates trust and openness thereby further solidifying the links with the unit, the noncommissioned officers and their heritage. The enlightened diamond wearer knows that the failure to properly manage conflict is a failure to facilitate the commander's ability to command.

Conclusion:

This most qualified soldier might be a wearer of the diamond, but until he or she is totally committed body (physical fitness), mind (social-psychologically) and soul (ethicist), he or she is not a first sergeant. The leadership culture of the unit (activity) to a great degree is defined by the first sergeant's reflected values, attitude, beliefs, language and behavioral patterns. It is from this culture that the unit grows in the spirit of the diamond.

The diamond wearer must use that trained ear to hear the "silent cries" of discontentment and dissatisfaction but respond often

116

times using the professional energies of the unit's leadership groups rather than solving the problems and disconnects. Training junior leaders include training them to listen for those "silent cries."

Therefore, the diamond wearer's leadership agenda is constructed based on the state of the unit's profiles. The profiles once assessed allows the wearer to better facilitate the commander's ability to command. The diamond wearer understands how and where all the duties, responsibilities and requirements of the unit's leadership groups intersect to produce the desired results. The wearer look through the complexities of the command process and separate the wheat from the chaff. The diamond wearer must never take lightly the awesome load that he or she bears. Hopefully, the chain of command will always fully support the first sergeant in the performance of the specified, directed, or implied duties.

The diamond wearer never allows procrastination to drain the creative energy or rob the wearer of the one quality that matters most in leadership: the feeling of being in charge.

117

Index

About The Author

Command Sergeant Major (Ret.) Bobby Owens considers his leadership time as a first sergeant the hallmark of twenty-nine years of active military service. He further maintains that much of his military success was owed to those who wore the diamond during his developmental years. Twenty -nine years of active military service provided him many insights and understanding of the intricacies of enlisted leadership that he has always shared willingly. As a command sergeant major, he devoted numerous hours stressing the key roles that first sergeants play in the lives of the soldiers in their charge.